THE MANTLE
ADORNED

Imam al-Bûsîrî's *Burda*

Translated, with further poetic
Ornaments, by

Abdal Hakim Murad

THE QUILLIAM PRESS

Calligraphy: Betül Kırkan
Illumination: Ersan Perçem
Marbled Endpapers: Sadreddin Özçimi
Graphic Design: M. Sadik Kutlu
English Typography: Abdal Lateef Whiteman
Printed by: Mega Basım Yayın San. ve Tic. A.Ş. Istanbul, Turkey
Copyright ©2009 Abdal Hakim Murad
Artwork and calligraphy reproduced by kind permission of
Alvarlı Efe Hazretleri İlim ve Sosyal Hizmetler Vakfı, Istanbul.
Poetry by Riad Nourallah reproduced by kind permission of
The University Press of Maryland

ISBN 978 1 872038 15 5

The Quilliam Press Ltd.,
29 Clifton Road, London N3 2AS United Kingdom

CONTENTS

FOREWORD

GOD'S WORK IN the universe is poetic and musical. In everything He does, He superbly combines function with beauty. This is nowhere more clearly reflected than in His book and final religion, the Koran and Islam. The Koran, in its own inimitable way, is a poetical and musical text, its meaning conveyed in a lyric style which is to be chanted in the distinctive harmonic mode known as *Tajwid*. Five daily prayers reflect this poetic and musical dimension of Islam: the believer is enjoined to recite the poetic text of the Koran with the best possible voice he can summon. This develops his sensitivity towards beauty and yields a particular kind of subtle excellence in every aspect of his life. It also teaches that in one's speech and actions not only the content but also the form and the way it is presented must be nothing less than the best.

If such are the examples God sets before human beings in His creation and religion, then everything we do must also capture and reflect the poetic dimension of life and action. Probably this is what modern life lacks most, with its tendency to focus on expediency at the expense of calmness and beauty. Even contemporary Muslims suffer from the lack of concern with the aesthetic, although it forms a part of Islam and of every traditional Islamic culture.

A classic example of beauty in meaning and form is the *Qasíde-i Burda* of Busiri, which you hold in your hands. In this new version, Abdal Hakim Murad has rendered it into English and has collected echoes of it as expressed by other hearts in various tongues around the world. The collection

demonstrates that love of beauty is universal. So is the language of love. For Busiri's poem is a eulogy of the most beautiful person who ever lived, 'unrivalled in both his character and in his physical appearance': the Prophet Muhammad, upon whom be peace. Busiri does this with poetry that seeks to be worthy of its subject. For centuries now, the *Mantle-Ode* has been a wellspring of blessing and healing for wounded hearts and minds. So will it be today.

I congratulate Abdal Hakim Murad for reproducing it in such beautiful English, and I commend also the calligrapher Betül Kırkan, and others from the atelier of the master-calligrapher of modern Turkey, Hüseyin Kutlu, who have worked so hard to adorn the pages of this production.

The Prophet ﷺ has said that God is beautiful, and that He loves beauty. *Allahu Jamil wa yuhibbu al-jamâl.* May God help us attain beauty in all the actions we humbly present to Him—just as the producers of this book have so impressively done.

RECEP ŞENTÜRK
1429/2008
ÇENGELKÖY, ISTANBUL

INTRODUCTION
PROPHETIC PRAISE POETRY

WHEREVER ISLAM TRAVELS, poetry seems to follow. At its very origin, the new religion exerted a dramatic impact on literature. The founder of Islam, while not himself a poet, supported poets in his community, and some of his Companions, such as Hassan ibn Thâbit, seem to have pioneered the sudden diversification and enlivening of Arabic literature which followed the rise of Islam. In due course, something similar happened to the other literatures touched by Muslim belief, as the Persian, Turkish, Swahili and many other peoples quickly found a new and exalted poetic voice with which to celebrate their faith, until Islam became, perhaps, the poetic civilisation *par excellence*. With its distinctive vision of language as ennobled by its ability to carry a word-for-word revelation of God's speech, Islamic culture always favoured the spoken word as the highest form of artistic expression. One might even say that above architecture, calligraphy and abstract decoration, poetry has been acknowledged as the highest Islamic art.

Each genuinely Muslim poem is, by definition, a 'handful from the sea' of the Messenger ﷺ. The soul of the Holy Prophet overflows down the centuries. Seen in dreams, studied in devotional chronicles, emulated in every detail of life, the object of the gratitude of millions saved from vice and the forgetting of God, the Prophet is acknowledged as the fountainhead (*serçeşme*) of Muslim happiness. Hence the universal Muslim practice of sealing every prayer, in every mosque, with the 'Benediction of Abraham', which calls down blessings and peace upon the Final Prophet, Abraham's heir through Ishmael. Other formulas of Prophetic benediction are too many to be counted; rooted in the Koran and Hadith, they have filled the Muslim life with a sense of intimacy and closeness to the religion's founder, the pattern of whose life for God they struggle to emulate. 'Bless the Prophet!' is an exclamation used in every Muslim language to quieten a quarrel, as it calls Muslims back to the memory of the man who stilled the ancient feuds of Arabia, and launched a civilisation that would unite races and languages in a single fellowship.

The 'Blessing on the Prophet', or the 'Prayer on the Prophet' (durûd şerif), is thus one of the most fundamental Muslim acts. The Koran itself enjoins it, in a verse which for centuries has been heard from Friday pulpits across Turkey and elsewhere:

> God and His angels send blessings upon the Prophet. O you who believe: send blessings upon him, and abundant peace! (33:56)

The 'prayer on the Prophet', as Molla Hüsrev explains, is ultimately for our benefit: the Prophet's rank in God's sight is already established at 'the Degree of Two Bows' Length'; but by joining the cosmic litany which blesses his perfection, we benefit spiritually; because for each utterance of praise and benediction, God blesses us tenfold. In this way he continues to benefit his community, and quench their spiritual thirst.

The durûd has a further, cosmic benefit. It links, in a loving and intimate way, the words 'Muhammad is God's Messenger' to the ultimate statement of the mystery of God: 'no god but God'. By closing each of the believer's five daily prayers, it eases the transition between the God-centredness of formal worship and the God-centredness of our ethical duties in the world. The Holy Prophet, bearer of the uncreated speech of God, returns from the heavenly experience of his Ascension, back to help and guide his people in the midst of their worldly concerns. As Nizami says:

> Canopy of nine thrones, above the seventh star,
> End and precious gemstone of Prophecy's long hour;
> The motes upon Muhammad's feet are wisdom blazing far
> His saddle-strap leads both the worlds, the glory of Allah.

And again:

He read the Book's own decalogue of courtesy,
Asking leave of all the Prophets to pass by.
His footsteps tore the curtain of the galaxy
His flag on seraph shoulders lifted high.

The lesson is clear: the Muslim is not to remain isolated in supernatural glory, but is to draw strength from the experience of God's presence to deal with the challenges of ordinary life. The glory of the Prophet, as every believer understands, is that he looked upon God, and therefore appreciated the pure finitude of creation; but still chose to live, work, and struggle for justice in the world, living with the poor and dispossessed. As Ahmed Shawqî puts it:

Were the classes of humanity to choose their religions
The poor would single your religion out among the rest.

And for the saint of Ankara, Hacı Bayram:

'Poverty is my pride! Poverty is my pride!'
Spake he not thus, of all the worlds the pride?
His poverty recall! His poverty recall!
This soul of mine is naughted deep within that pride.

Hacı Bayram is telling us here that contemplating the Prophet's life of poverty and prayer is essential to our spiritual health. Our souls, imagining his absolute single-heartedness, become aware of their absentness, their distraction and their greed. His every hour was a campaign against the ego, both within the soul and in the unjust, tyrannical structures of the world. Choosing poverty for himself, he challenged the Pharoahs and the Caesars who exploited the poor and the weak. As the prophets of earlier times well knew, prophetic religion is a total commitment.

The Prophet's birth is thus the birth of freedom, a 'glorious proclamation.' The miracles surrounding his birth, which the earliest Muslim chroniclers record, are 'good news and a warning': good news to the poor and the weak, and a warning to those whose blind selfishness is destroying the order of God's world.

> For the love of him who cometh turns the sky,
> Yearning for his face do men and angels sigh.
> He who cometh is that King, the Prophets' Seal,
> He, that 'Mercy to the Worlds', Creation's weal.

SÜLEYMAN ÇELEBI

For this reason, perhaps the most popular of the subgenres of Prophetic panegyric is the long poem which focuses entirely on the *mevlit (maulid)*, the 'night when guidance was born'. As Harvard University's Annemarie Schimmel records:

> The number of poems written for this festive occasion in all Islamic languages is beyond reckoning. From the eastern end of the Muslim world to the west, the *maulid* is a wonderful occasion for the pious to show their warm love of the Prophet in songs, poems, and prayers. Nowhere has the simple trust in the grace of the Prophet and his intercession at Doomsday been expressed more beautifully than in Turkey, where Süleyman Çelebi (d.1419) told the story of Muhammad's birth in his *Mevlûd-i şerif*, a *mathnawî* in touchingly unsophisticated Turkish verse of the simplest possible meter, to which is added a sweet melody.

Süleyman Çelebi's poem is probably second only to Busiri's 'Mantle-Ode' in its popularity. Its huge effectiveness may be experienced by those who attend the annual *maulid* festival at the Bosnian town of Blagaj, where over twenty thousand lovers of the Prophet spend the night beneath the moon, listening to exquisitely sung praise-poems, culminating in a recital of Süleyman Çelebi's ancient words.

A second summit of the genre is poetry which celebrates the Prophetic Intercession (*şefaat*), when, at the Judgement-Day, the Blessed Prophet will intercede for the sinners of the world. According to a hadith, the Prophet himself described this as follows:

> I go before the Throne, and fall down in prostration before my Lord. Then God inspires in me such praises and great glorification

of Him as were never inspired in anyone before me, and it is said: 'O Muhammad! Lift up your head! Ask, and you will be answered; plead for intercession, and it will be granted you.' So I raise my head and say: 'My nation! My nation!' And I am told: 'O Muhammad! Bring in those of your nation for whom there need be no reckoning by the right-hand Gate of Heaven! The remaining Gates shall be for the others.'

Thus does the Prophet ﷺ appear most superbly as 'God's Beloved', *habibullâh*; and on the basis of this and many other hadiths, a huge literature arose celebrating humanity's forgiveness through the Prophetic intercession:

> On the gate of thy bounty this sinning head leans,
> Distraught by his love, O blessed of face!
> He hopes for God's pardon with you as his means,
> He fears Heaven's anger, damp tears on his face.
>
> IBN HAJAR AL-ASQALANI

Today, praise-poems seem to be more popular than ever. Love of the Prophet ﷺ has spilled over into new genres, such as film, theatre and the novel; but wherever Muslims gather for poetic celebrations, the Prophet is likely to be at the centre of the poet's interest. The present volume includes a few scraps and fragments from this burgeoning and often highly-innovative literature.

IMAM BUSIRI

Muhammad ibn Sa'id al-Busiri was born in the Upper Egyptian village of Behnesa in 1212, to a poor family of Moroccan Berber origin. After memorising the Koran and other holy texts he travelled to Cairo, where he continued his education. Employed as a clerk and magistrate in several towns of the Nile Delta, he wrote several poems praising local governors, while condemning commercial malpractices and the obstinacy of debtors. His religious sensibility seems to have grown slowly, and his elegy on the death of his teacher, the Sufi spiritual guide Abu'l-Abbas al-Mursi, shows an increasing attachment to the devotional life. His contemporary Ibn 'Ata'illah of Alexandria (d.1309) advocated a path of passionate mystical love, and this probably accounts for many of the more emotional verses for which his great poem, the *Burda*, is famous. His physical feebleness, his many children, and an apparently difficult wife, ensured that his financial situation was often insecure; and when he suffered a stroke in middle age, his situation seemed desperate. Hardly able to speak or to hold a pen, he still managed to express his love for the Prophet ﷺ in heartfelt verse, a devotion which was rewarded when, according to the historians, the Prophet ﷺ appeared to him in a dream, and placed his mantle (*burda*) upon his shoulders. On waking, Busiri found that his health had been miraculously restored. He went on to live a full life, and died in Cairo or Alexandria, perhaps in 1297. In the latter city, his mosque and tomb stand opposite the great mosque-complex of his teacher al-Mursi. His small but charming mosque was renovated and expanded by Mehmet Sait Paşa in 1864, and its walls boast, in addition to 94 verses of the *Burda* executed in the Nasta'liq script, other exquisitely calligraphed poems in Arabic and Turkish.

THE BURDA

As Professor Schimmel notes, the 'Mantle-Ode' is 'the favourite poem of Muslims everywhere'. Formally entitled 'Glittering Stars in Praise of the Best of Creation,' it takes a strongly classical form, beginning with the ancient Arabian theme of the lover soliloquizing amid the remains of his lost beloved's encampment. Even here, however, we soon realise that the loved one is not a Bedouin maiden, but is none other than *Habibullâh*, 'God's Beloved'. The Blessed Prophet has died, and the world is bereft in his absence; but there is still hope. We are exiled from beauty only by our own ugliness, and therefore the poet must bewail the waywardness of his ego's desires. This leads to a realisation of the perfection of the Prophet ﷺ, whose moral and spiritual qualities were in precisely that state of harmony which the poet craves. By considering the miracles which accompanied the Prophet's birth, he feels hope and gratitude to God; by considering his many miracles his faith is strengthened, and by pondering the deep wisdom of the Koran, the mysterious 'bride' which the believer must slowly and courteously unveil, he is reminded of the meaning of history. The poem then turns to consider the Ascension (*mi'raj*), the climax of the Prophet's ﷺ career, in which he was carried from the Mosque of Jerusalem up through the seven heavens into the divine presence. Returning, he risks life and limb by heroically defending his people against pagans who have attacked their refuge in Medina. Busiri then laments his own sinfulness and his declining years, and yearns for the blessing of the Prophet's intercession on the day of Judgement. He knows that given his ruinous and repeated sins, only God can save him; and so he addresses the Messenger ﷺ, whose prayers and intercessions are, as the hadith assure us, to be the surest mediator with God. Finally, he prays for gentleness in this world and the next, ending with a brief allusion to the Arabian scenery with which he began.

Despite the difficulty of the ode's very exalted Arabic, the *Burda* has attracted more devotional and literary attention than any other Muslim poem. (Some even claim it to be the most widely-memorised poem in the world.) One sign of this has been its abundant use in architecture. The Topkapı Palace in Istanbul, the potent symbol of Muslim power and civilisation for five centuries, and whose treasures include the original mantle of the Prophet, is adorned everywhere with Iznik tiles carrying the text of the *Burda*. The same poem may be seen on the walls of the great private homes of Aleppo and Baghdad (and some particularly fine examples adorn the famous Suheimi House in Cairo). Mosques from Marrakech to Jakarta carry verses from the text, or even the entire poem; a particularly good example is a band of cartouches in the nineteenth-century Muhammad Ali Mosque in Cairo, which dominates the city's skyline. Saladin's tomb in Damascus is decorated with verse 34. The *Burda* is also found in innumerable fine examples of ceramics and embroidery: line 135 was stitched upon the banner of the great 19th-century Algerian independence leader Abdel Kader.

The poem has been widely imitated, in the so-called 'Road of the *Burda*' (*Nahj al-Burda*) genre. A celebrated example is the poem by ʿAʾisha al-Baʿuniyya of Damascus (d.1516), regarded as a showcase of elaborate Arabic style. Perhaps the most popular example known today is by the Cairene Ahmed Shawqî (d.1932).

Hundreds of commentaries exist on the poem, of which Ömer Harputi's *Asidat al-Shuhda* (*Essence of the Honeycomb*) has been used in preparing this translation. The Persian commentary by Jalal al-Din Yusuf also offers a helpful window into the obscurer linguistic and spiritual mysteries of the poem. Further, Muslim poets have adorned the *Burda* with what is known as *tashtir*: interlinear augmentations maintaining the original metre and rhyme. The *Burda* is also said to be the most popular subject in Islamic literature for the genre of *takhmisas*, which add three further hemistiches to each two-hemistich line. Among the most famous is the poem of Abbas Efendi, 'Solace in Solitude'. As with the commentaries, these extended poetic versions often seek to bring to the surface the hidden symbolism which many have found in the poem.

Although educated Muslims everywhere have usually known Arabic well (even though only a small percentage of Muslims worldwide are native speakers), translations of the *Burda*, preserving its original metre and rhyme, are abundant. In Turkish, the best-known is perhaps the elaborate version of the Istanbul chief judge Kemâl Paşa-zâde (d.1534), but other translations are easily available in local bookshops. In Persian, the poet Abd al-Rahman Jami (d. 1492) composed a brilliant translation which then formed the basis for further poetic elaborations and commentaries. In the Subcontinent, Jami's translation, with an Urdu commentary, is still widely read among educated people, and sung in public gatherings. In the Malay world, an anonymous 16th century translation is thought to be the first book known to have been translated into Malay from any language. In Africa, many versions exist in Swahili, Fulfulde, Wolof, Hausa, Peul, Mandinka, and Somali, all written in Arabic letters. In Chinese, Ma An-Li's three-volume translation and commentary was published in Shanghai in 1890. The best-known Bosnian version is by the nineteenth-century Halil Hrle of Stolac; traditional Albanian readers were served by Muhamet Kyçyku (d.1844) and others. The first Kazan Tatar commentary was published in 1847.

Translations into Western European languages began in 1771 with the Latin version of Johannes Uri. The first German translation came in 1824, while René Basset's *La Bordah du Cheikh al-Bousiri* (Paris, 1894) is not the first, but is probably the most successful poetic version in French. The first English translation appeared in 1881 at the hands of James Redhouse, author of the great *Turkish-English Lexicon*, while the most impressive remains that of Hamza Yusuf (2004), which is accompanied by a set of CD audio recordings of the celebrated Fez Singers, performing in traditional 'Andalusian' style. The present translation owes much to Yusuf's gifted rendering.

I have added to my own version an implicit poetic commentary. Prophetic panegyric is the largest genre in Muslim religious poetry; and from this enormous ocean I have tried to select verses which affirm, clarify, or extend Busiri's insights. As this is an English translation, there is a disproportionate reliance on Anglophone poets. Abdullah Quilliam and Yahya Parkinson are the obvious choices, but I have also added a few extracts from versified plays, such as Amherst Tyssen's *Birth of Islam* (1895) and Wilfred Scawen Blunt's *Bride of the Nile* (1907). But the great medievals of the East are present also, including Rumi, the Anatolian sage who is now among the most popular poets in the world. The more complex symbolic poetry, which itself requires commentary, has been avoided; however I have tried to present a fair sample of the different cultural styles, from the simple pieties of Süleyman Çelebi to the baroque elaborations of Nâbî. Non-Muslims are also represented, particularly Goethe, whose *Mahomets-Gesang* (1772), set twice to music by Schubert, is only one of his great celebrations of Muslim faith. Fragments of Victor Hugo's unjustly-neglected poem *L'An Neuf de l'Hégire* are also included.

The Mantle Adorned may serve, it is hoped, as an aid to devotion. In the traditional manner, each line, and the *nazira* lines which follow, should be the subject of an hour's quiet meditation. Blessing the Prophet, and indeed all of the prophets and saints, brings a blessing to our lives, and stillness to the heart. 'Whoever blesses me once,' he says, 'shall be blessed tenfold by God.'

ABDAL HAKIM MURAD
4 Rebi' ül-Evvel, 1429

The Rose of Medina   *Cahide Keskiner*

امِنْ تَذَكُّرِ جِيرَانٍ بِذِى سَلَمِ

مَزَجْتَ دَمْعًا جَرَى مِنْ مُقْلَةٍ بِدَمِ

1. *Is it from remembering past neighbours at*
Dhû Salam* that you mingle with blood
tears shed from your eyes?

Stop at the halting-places
Near Mecca's holy places,
Seek out the Prophet's traces -
With dust anoint your cheek.

IBN DAQÎQ AL-ʿID

* *A mythical desert rendezvous of lovers.*

17

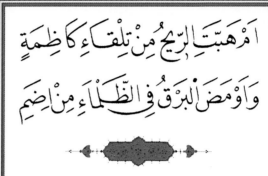

اَمْ هَبَّتَ الرِّيحُ مِنْ تِلْقَاءِ كَاظِمَةٍ

وَاَوْمَضَ الْبَرْقُ فِى الظَّلْمَاءِ مِنْ اِضَمِ

2. Or has the wind blown from before
Kâzima,* and the lightning flashed
in Idam's** dark?

Light the darkest realms of error
  With Islamic truth and right,
Even as the lord Muhammed
  Lit Arabia's darkest night.

YAHYA PARKINSON

* A name of the City of Medina.
** A mountain near the City.

18

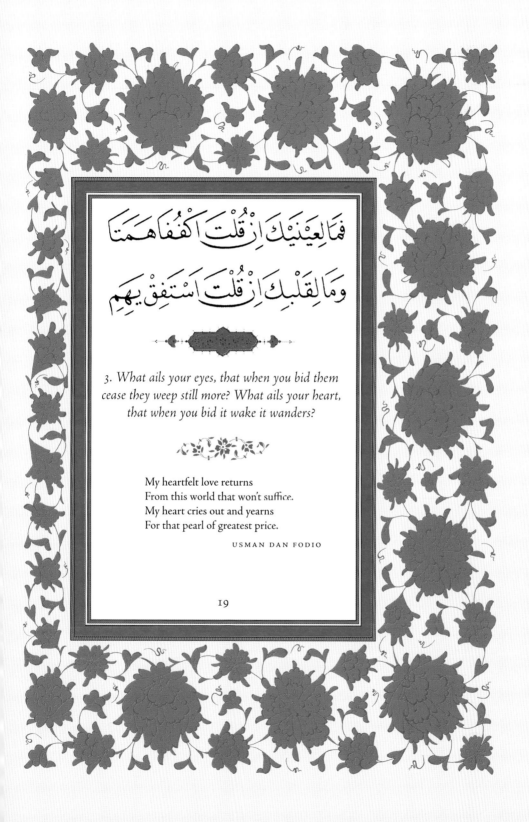

فَمَا لِعَيْنَيْكَ اِنْ قُلْتَ اكْفُفَاهُمَتَا

وَمَا لِقَلْبِكَ اِنْ قُلْتَ اسْتَفِقْ يَهِمِ

3. What ails your eyes, that when you bid them
cease they weep still more? What ails your heart,
that when you bid it wake it wanders?

My heartfelt love returns
From this world that won't suffice.
My heart cries out and yearns
For that pearl of greatest price.

USMAN DAN FODIO

19

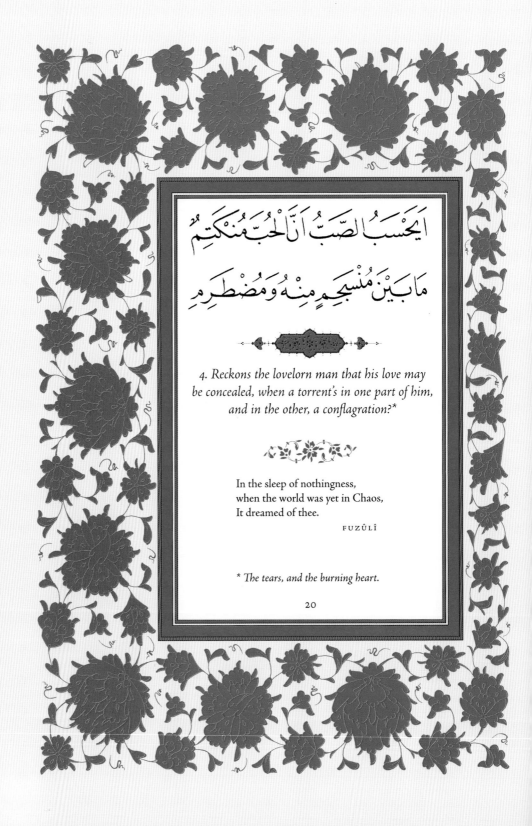

ايَحْسَبُ الصَّبُّ اَنَّ الْحُبَّ مُنْكَتِمُ

مَابَيْنَ مُنْسَجِمٍ مِنْهُ وَمُضْطَرِمِ

4. Reckons the lovelorn man that his love may
be concealed, when a torrent's in one part of him,
and in the other, a conflagration?*

In the sleep of nothingness,
when the world was yet in Chaos,
It dreamed of thee.

FUZÛLÎ

* The tears, and the burning heart.

20

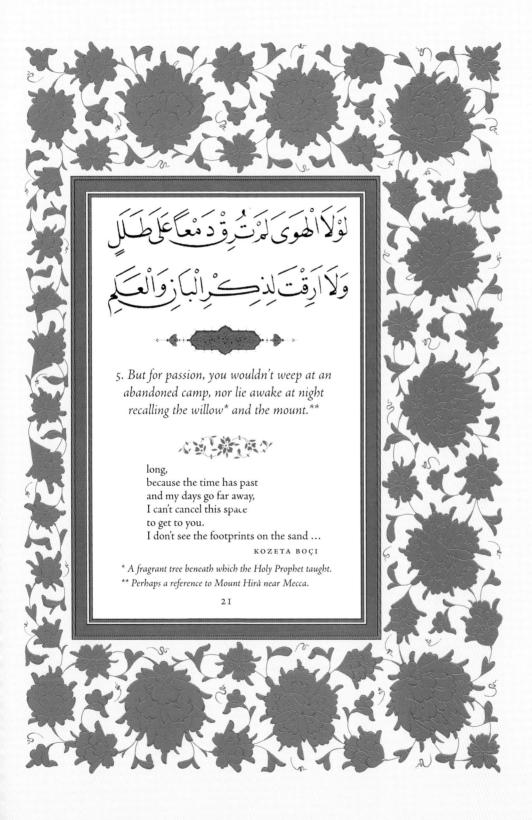

لَوْلَا الْهَوَى لَمْ تُرِقْ دَمْعًا عَلَى طَلَلِ

وَلَا أَرِقْتَ لِذِكْرِ الْبَانِ وَالْعَلَمِ

5. But for passion, you wouldn't weep at an
abandoned camp, nor lie awake at night
recalling the willow* and the mount.**

long,
because the time has past
and my days go far away,
I can't cancel this space
to get to you.
I don't see the footprints on the sand …
KOZETA BOÇI

* A fragrant tree beneath which the Holy Prophet taught.
** Perhaps a reference to Mount Hirâ near Mecca.

21

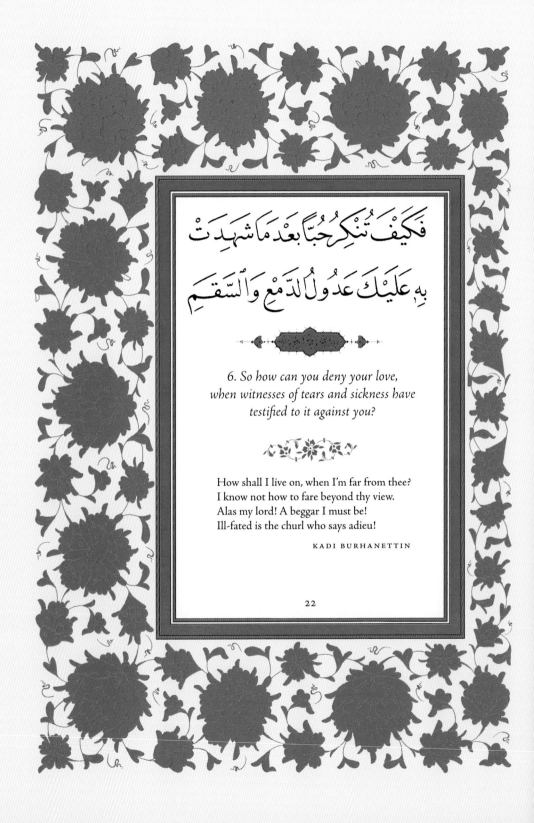

فَكَيْفَ تُنْكِرُ حُبًّا بَعْدَ مَا شَهِدَتْ

بِهِ عَلَيْكَ عُدُولُ الدَّمْعِ وَالسَّقَمِ

6. So how can you deny your love,
when witnesses of tears and sickness have
testified to it against you?

How shall I live on, when I'm far from thee?
I know not how to fare beyond thy view.
Alas my lord! A beggar I must be!
Ill-fated is the churl who says adieu!

KADI BURHANETTIN

22

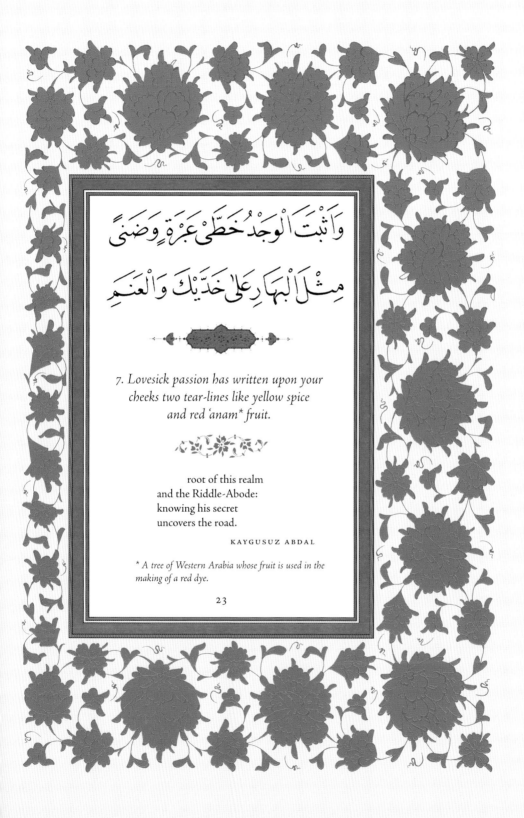

وَاَثْبَتَ الْوَجْدُ خَطَّىٰ عَبْرَةٍ وَضَنَّىٰ

مِثْلَ الْبَهَارِ عَلَىٰ خَدَّيْكَ وَالْغَنَمِ

7. *Lovesick passion has written upon your*
cheeks two tear-lines like yellow spice
and red 'anam* fruit.

root of this realm
and the Riddle-Abode:
knowing his secret
uncovers the road.

KAYGUSUZ ABDAL

* A tree of Western Arabia whose fruit is used in the
making of a red dye.

23

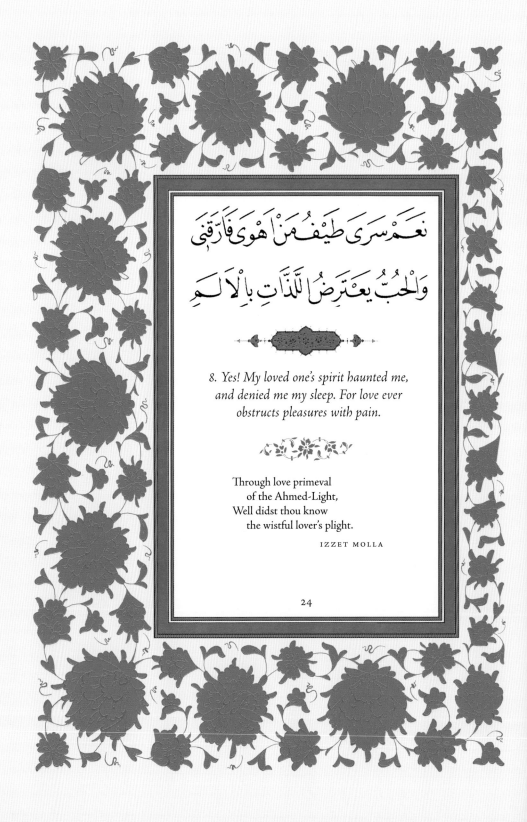

نَعَمْ سَرَى طَيْفُ مَنْ هَوَى فَأَرَّقَنِي

وَالْحُبُّ يَعْتَرِضُ اللَّذَّاتِ بِالْاَلَمِ

8. Yes! My loved one's spirit haunted me,
and denied me my sleep. For love ever
obstructs pleasures with pain.

Through love primeval
of the Ahmed-Light,
Well didst thou know
the wistful lover's plight.

IZZET MOLLA

24

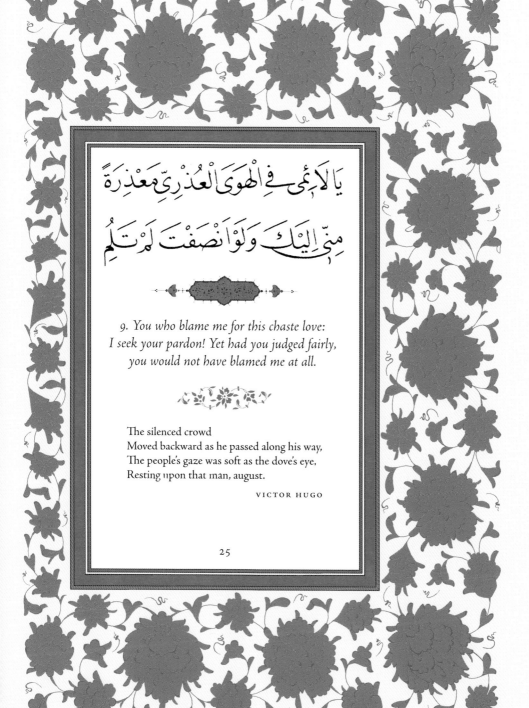

يَا لَائِمِي فِي الْهَوَى الْعُذْرِيِّ مَعْذِرَةً

مِنِّي إِلَيْكَ وَلَوْ أَنْصَفْتَ لَمْ تَلُمِ

9. You who blame me for this chaste love:
I seek your pardon! Yet had you judged fairly,
you would not have blamed me at all.

The silenced crowd
Moved backward as he passed along his way,
The people's gaze was soft as the dove's eye,
Resting upon that man, august.

VICTOR HUGO

25

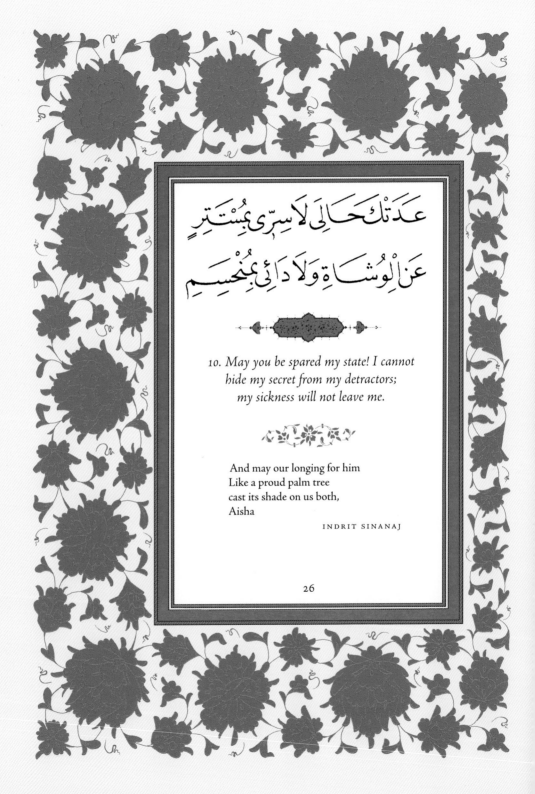

عَدَتْكَ حَالِي لَا سِرِّي بِمُسْتَتِرٍ
عَنِ الوُشَاةِ وَلَا دَائِي بِمُنْحَسِمِ

10. *May you be spared my state! I cannot*
hide my secret from my detractors;
my sickness will not leave me.

And may our longing for him
Like a proud palm tree
cast its shade on us both,
Aisha

INDRIT SINANAJ

26

محضّتني النّصح لكن لست أسمعه
انّ المحبّ عن العذّال في صمم

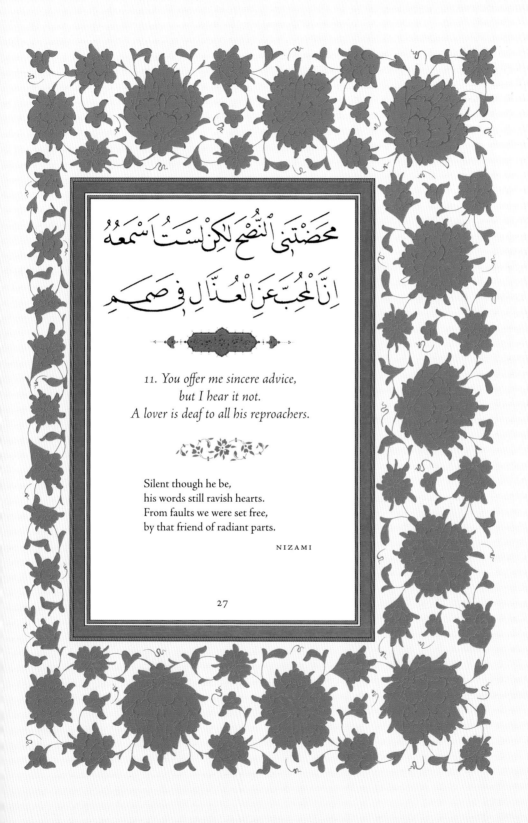

11. *You offer me sincere advice,*
but I hear it not.
A lover is deaf to all his reproachers.

Silent though he be,
his words still ravish hearts.
From faults we were set free,
by that friend of radiant parts.

NIZAMI

27

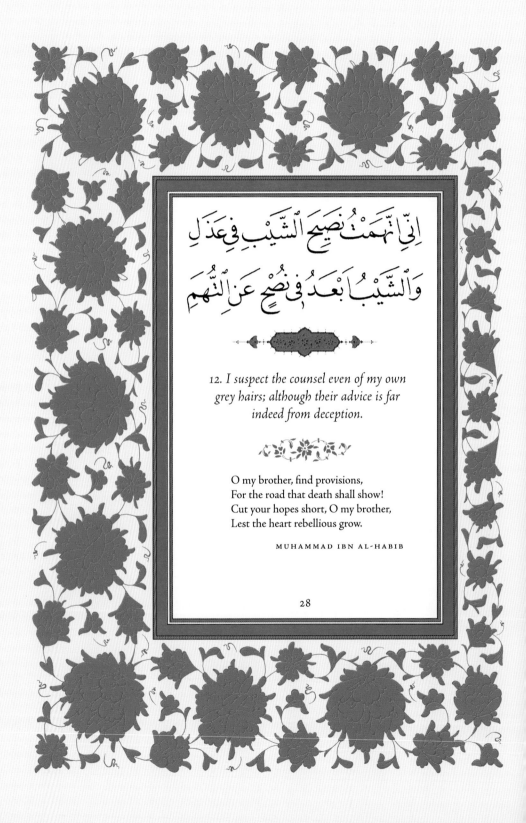

اِنِّى اتَّهَمْتُ نَصِيحَ الشَّيْبِ فِى عَذَلِ
وَالشَّيْبُ اَبْعَدُ فِى نُصْحٍ عَنِ التُّهَمِ

12. *I suspect the counsel even of my own grey hairs; although their advice is far indeed from deception.*

O my brother, find provisions,
For the road that death shall show!
Cut your hopes short, O my brother,
Lest the heart rebellious grow.

MUHAMMAD IBN AL-HABIB

28

فَإِنْ آمَارَتِي بِالسُّوءِ مَا اتَّعَظَتْ

مِنْ جَهْلِهَا بِنَذِيرِ الشَّيْبِ وَالْهَرَمِ

13. *Thanks to its foolishness, my ill-urging
ego has paid no heed to the warner:
white hair and decrepitude.*

Never do I find myself
in the routs of joyfulness,
Since my head is always high
with the wine Forgetfulness.

HIBATULLAH IŞÂN

29

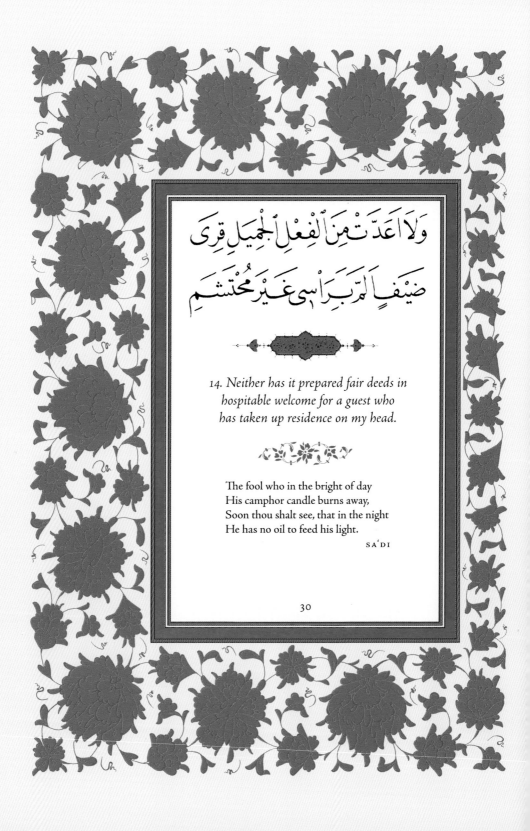

ولَا اَعَدَّتْ مِنَ الْفِعْلِ الْجَمِيلِ قِرَى

ضَيْفٍ الَمَّ بِرَأْسِى غَيْرُ مُحْتَشِم

14. Neither has it prepared fair deeds in
hospitable welcome for a guest who
has taken up residence on my head.

The fool who in the bright of day
His camphor candle burns away,
Soon thou shalt see, that in the night
He has no oil to feed his light.

SAʻDI

30

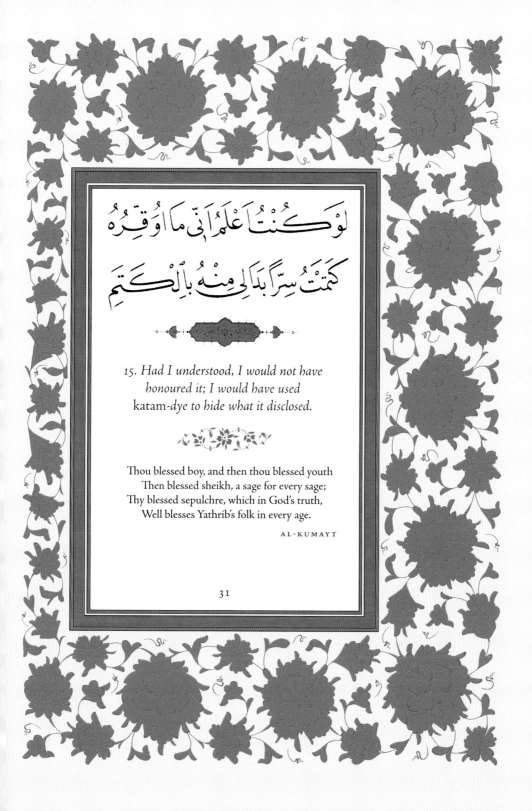

لَوْ كُنْتَ أَعْلَمُ أَنِّى مَا أُوَقِّرُهُ

كَتَمْتُ سِرًّا بَدَا لِى مِنْهُ بِالْكَتَمِ

15. Had I understood, I would not have
honoured it; I would have used
katam-dye to hide what it disclosed.

Thou blessed boy, and then thou blessed youth
Then blessed sheikh, a sage for every sage;
Thy blessed sepulchre, which in God's truth,
Well blesses Yathrib's folk in every age.

AL-KUMAYT

31

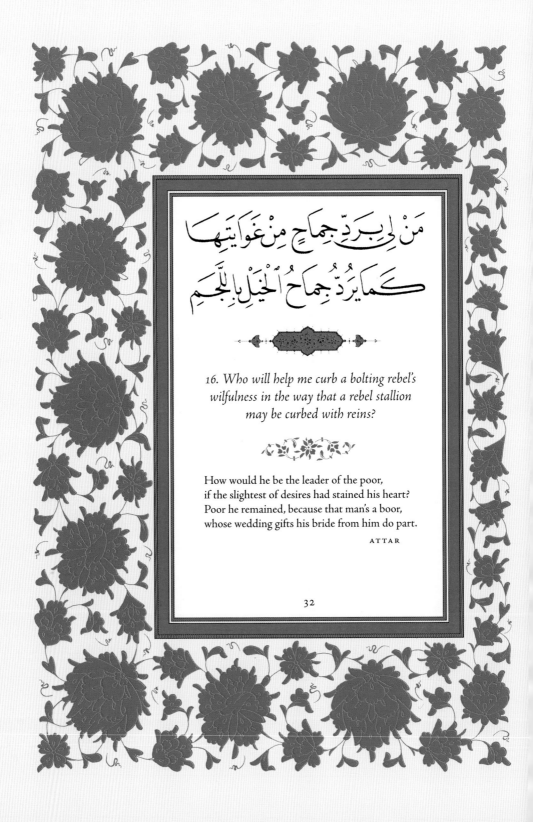

مَنْ لِي بِرَدِّ جِمَاحٍ مِنْ غِوَايَتِهَا
كَمَا يَرُدُّ جِمَاحُ الْخَيْلِ بِاللَّجَمِ

16. Who will help me curb a bolting rebel's
wilfulness in the way that a rebel stallion
may be curbed with reins?

How would he be the leader of the poor,
if the slightest of desires had stained his heart?
Poor he remained, because that man's a boor,
whose wedding gifts his bride from him do part.

ATTAR

32

فَلَا تَرُمْ بِالْمَعَاصِى كَسْرَ شَهْوَتِهَا
اِنَّ الطَّعَامَ يُقَوِّى شَهْوَةَ النَّهِمِ

17. *Think not to break unlawful whims*
by satisfying them.
Food only increases a glutton's desires.

Can pleasures heal the illness
of the soul which they have harmed?
Can pleasures offer stillness
to the mind?

MUHAMMAD JAMÂL AL-RIFA'I

33

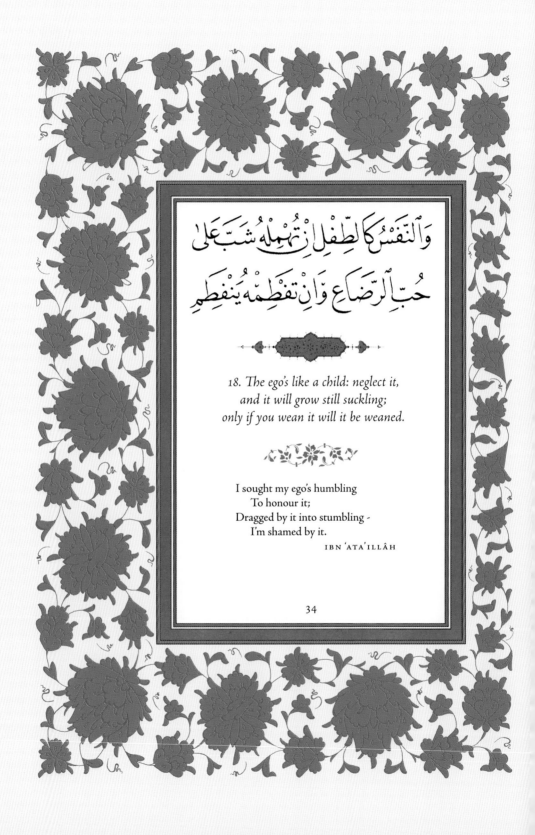

وَالنَّفْسُ كَالطِّفْلِ اِنْ تُهْمِلْهُ شَبَّ عَلَى
حُبِّ الرَّضَاعِ وَاِنْ تَفْطِمْهُ يَنْفَطِمِ

18. *The ego's like a child: neglect it,*
and it will grow still suckling;
only if you wean it will it be weaned.

I sought my ego's humbling
To honour it;
Dragged by it into stumbling -
I'm shamed by it.

IBN ʿATAʾILLÂH

34

وَرَاعِهَا وَهِيَ فِي الْأَعْمَالِ سَائِمَةٌ

وَإِنْ هِيَ اسْتَحْلَتِ الْمَرْعَى فَلَا تَسِمْ

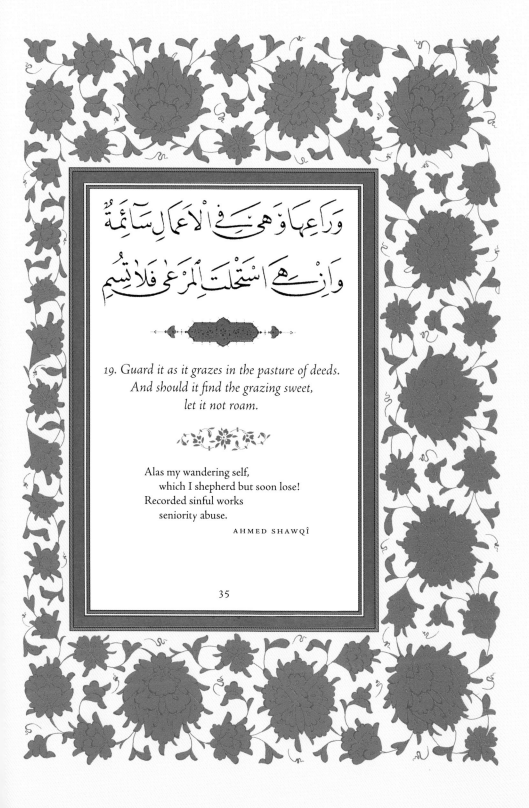

19. Guard it as it grazes in the pasture of deeds.
And should it find the grazing sweet,
let it not roam.

Alas my wandering self,
    which I shepherd but soon lose!
Recorded sinful works
    seniority abuse.

AHMED SHAWQÎ

35

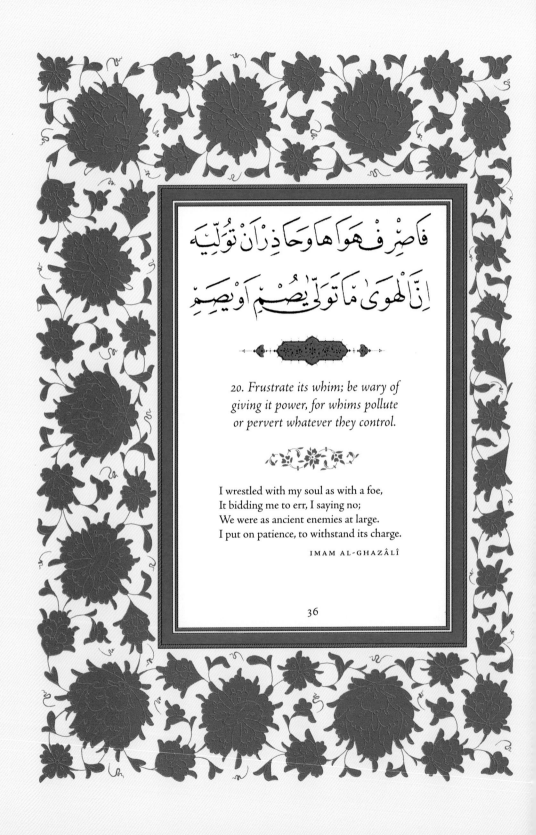

فَاصْرِفْ هَوَاهَا وَحَاذِرْ اَنْ تُوَلِّيَهَ
اِنَّ الْهَوَىٰ مَا تَوَلَّىٰ يُصْمِ اَوْ يَصِمِ

20. *Frustrate its whim; be wary of*
giving it power, for whims pollute
or pervert whatever they control.

I wrestled with my soul as with a foe,
It bidding me to err, I saying no;
We were as ancient enemies at large.
I put on patience, to withstand its charge.

IMAM AL-GHAZÂLÎ

36

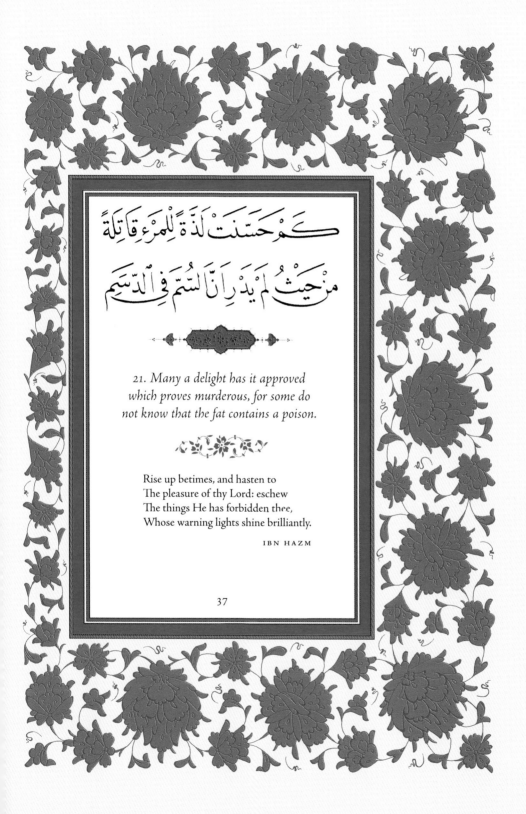

كَمْ حَسَّنَتْ لَذَّةً لِلْمَرْءِ قَاتِلَةً

مِنْ حَيْثُ لَمْ يَدْرِ اَنَّ السُّمَّ فِى الدَّسَمِ

21. Many a delight has it approved
which proves murderous, for some do
not know that the fat contains a poison.

Rise up betimes, and hasten to
The pleasure of thy Lord: eschew
The things He has forbidden thee,
Whose warning lights shine brilliantly.

IBN HAZM

37

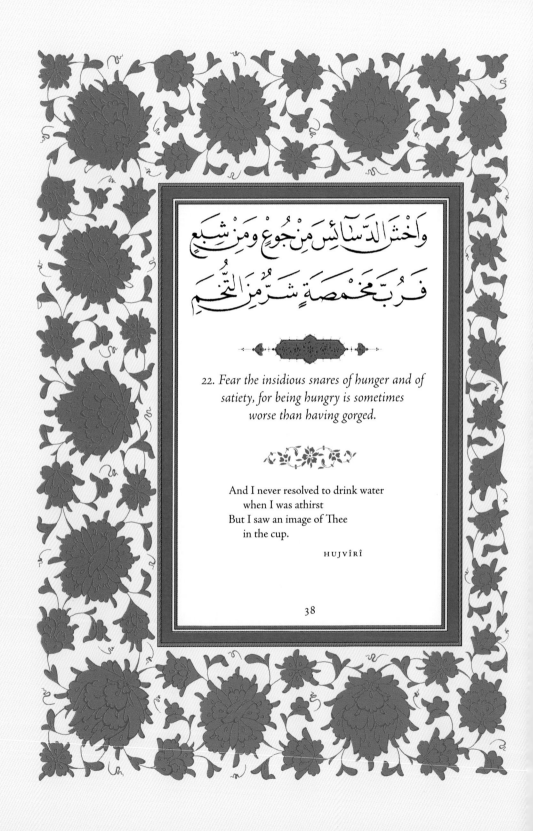

وَاخْشَ الدَّسَائِسَ مِنْ جُوعٍ وَمِنْ شِبَعٍ
فَرُبَّ مَخْمَصَةٍ شَرٌّ مِنَ التُّخَمِ

22. Fear the insidious snares of hunger and of
satiety, for being hungry is sometimes
worse than having gorged.

And I never resolved to drink water
when I was athirst
But I saw an image of Thee
in the cup.

HUJVÎRÎ

38

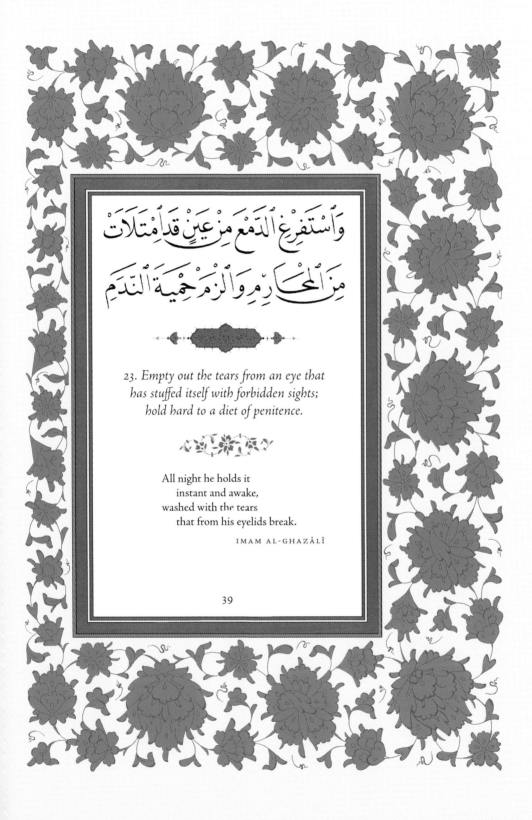

وَٱسْتَفْرِغِ ٱلدَّمْعَ مِنْ عَيْنٍ قَدِ ٱمْتَلَاتْ

مِنَ ٱلْمَحَارِمِ وَٱلْزَمْ حِمْيَةَ ٱلنَّدَمِ

23. *Empty out the tears from an eye that*
has stuffed itself with forbidden sights;
hold hard to a diet of penitence.

All night he holds it
instant and awake,
washed with the tears
that from his eyelids break.

IMAM AL-GHAZÂLÎ

39

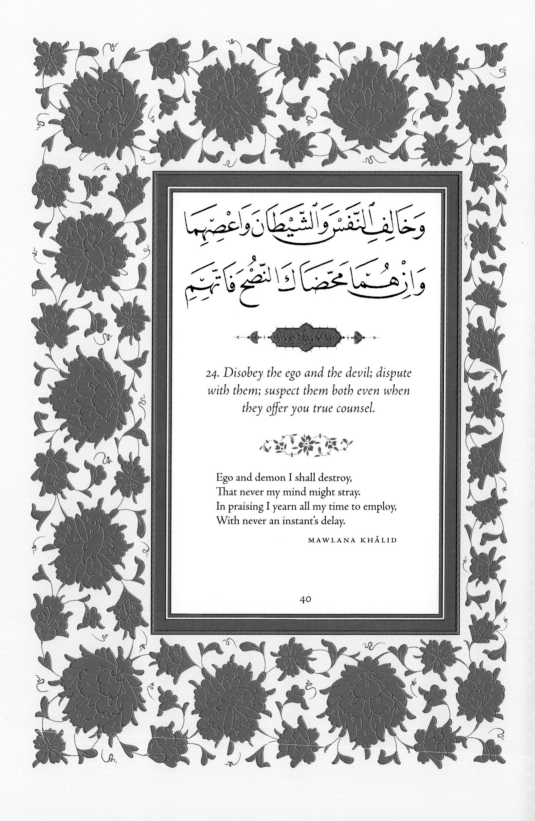

وَخَالِفِ النَّفْسَ وَالشَّيْطَانَ وَاعْصِهِمَا
وَإِنْ هُمَا مَحَّضَاكَ النُّصْحَ فَاتَّهِمِ

24. *Disobey the ego and the devil; dispute with them; suspect them both even when they offer you true counsel.*

Ego and demon I shall destroy,
That never my mind might stray.
In praising I yearn all my time to employ,
With never an instant's delay.

MAWLANA KHÂLID

40

وَلَا تُطِعْ مِنْهُمَا خَصْمًا وَلَا حَكَمًا

فَأَنْتَ تَعْرِفُ كَيْدَ الْخَصْمِ وَالْحَكَمِ

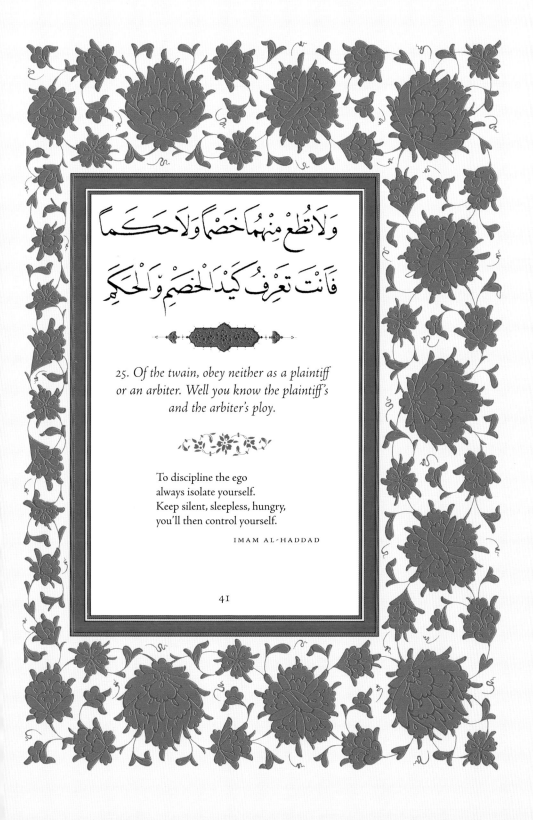

25. *Of the twain, obey neither as a plaintiff
or an arbiter. Well you know the plaintiff's
and the arbiter's ploy.*

To discipline the ego
always isolate yourself.
Keep silent, sleepless, hungry,
you'll then control yourself.

IMAM AL-HADDAD

41

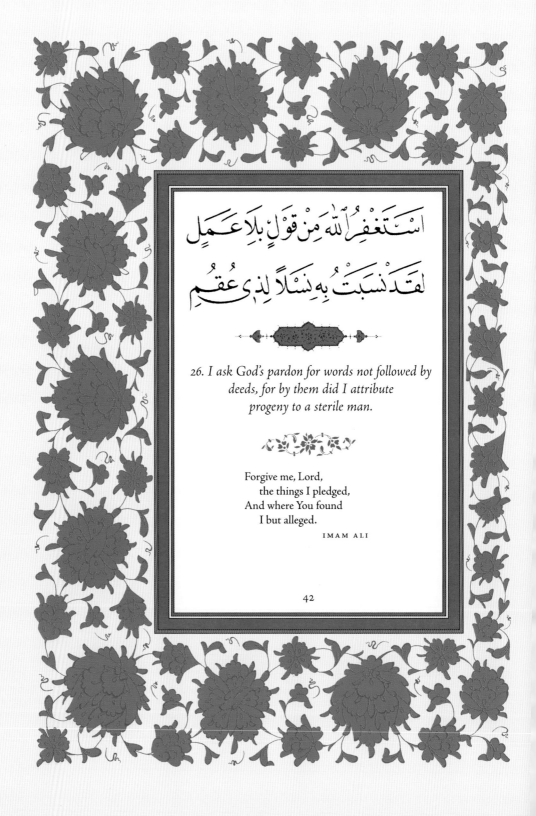

استَغْفِرُ اللهَ مِنْ قَوْلٍ بِلَا عَمَلِ

لَقَدْ نَسَبْتُ بِهِ نَسْلاً لِذِى عُقْمِ

26. I ask God's pardon for words not followed by
deeds, for by them did I attribute
progeny to a sterile man.

Forgive me, Lord,
   the things I pledged,
And where You found
   I but alleged.

IMAM ALI

42

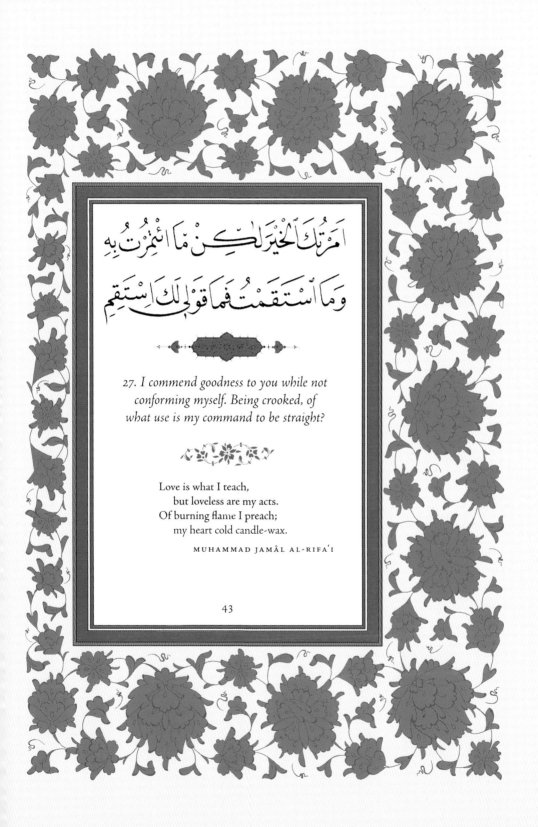

امَرْتُكَ الْخَيْرَ لَكِنْ مَا ائْتَمَرْتُ بِهِ
وَمَا اسْتَقَمْتُ فَمَا قَوْلِي لَكَ اسْتَقِمْ

27. *I commend goodness to you while not*
conforming myself. Being crooked, of
what use is my command to be straight?

Love is what I teach,
  but loveless are my acts.
Of burning flame I preach;
  my heart cold candle-wax.

MUHAMMAD JAMÂL AL-RIFA'I

43

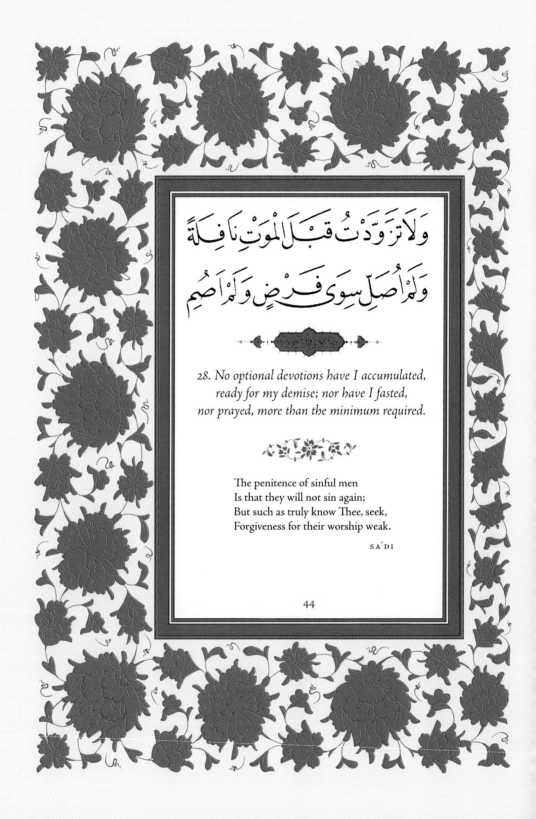

ولَا تَزَوَّدْتُ قَبْلَ الْمَوْتِ نَافِلَةً

وَلَمْ أُصَلِّ سِوَى فَرْضٍ وَلَمْ أَصُمِ

28. *No optional devotions have I accumulated,*
ready for my demise; nor have I fasted,
nor prayed, more than the minimum required.

The penitence of sinful men
Is that they will not sin again;
But such as truly know Thee, seek,
Forgiveness for their worship weak.

SA'DI

44

ظَلَمْتُ سُنَّةَ مَنْ أَحْيَا الظَّلَامَ إِلَى
اَنِ اشْتَكَتْ قَدَمَاهُ الضُّرَّ مِنْ وَرَمِ

29. *I've wronged the example of him who
revived the black nights, praying until his
feet complained of painful swelling.*

million lit windows
rise against
a treeless mountain
the Prophet prayed on.

PAUL SUTHERLAND

45

وَشَدَّ مِنْ سَغَبٍ حْشَاءَهُ وَطَوَى
تَحْتَ الْحِجَارَةِ كَشْحًا مُتْرَفَ الْأَدَمِ

30. Over his belly and soft skin he
placed a stone, tightening a belt over it
to lessen the hunger-pangs.

Because he had nothing, he sat on the sand;
Because he was hungry
        he tied stones to his waist.
Absolute poverty's proof was in him,
Absolute wealth was his secret within.

ATTAR

46

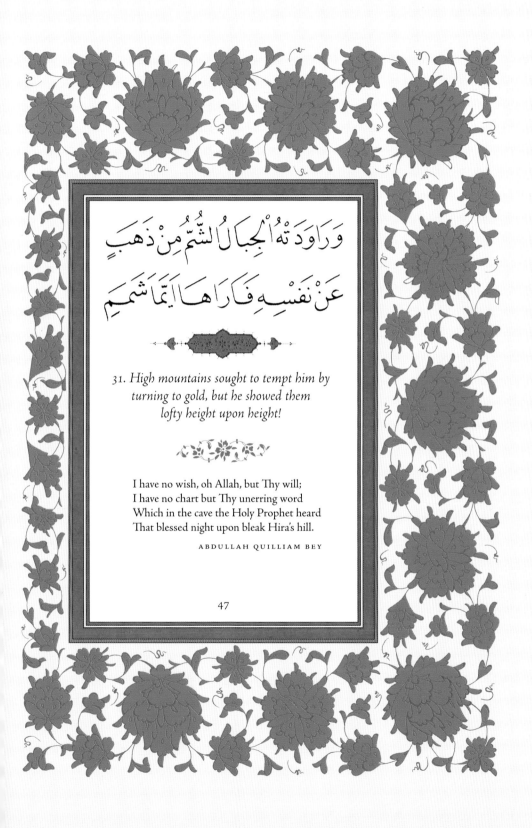

وَرَاوَدَتْهُ الْجِبَالُ الشُّمَّ مِنْ ذَهَبٍ

عَنْ نَفْسِهِ فَأَرَاهَا أَيُّمَا شَمَمِ

31. *High mountains sought to tempt him by*
    turning to gold, but he showed them
    lofty height upon height!

I have no wish, oh Allah, but Thy will;
I have no chart but Thy unerring word
Which in the cave the Holy Prophet heard
That blessed night upon bleak Hira's hill.

ABDULLAH QUILLIAM BEY

47

وَأَكَّدَتْ زُهْدَهُ فِيهَا ضَرُورَتُهُ

إِنَّ الضَّرُورَةَ لَاتَعْدُو عَلَى الْعِصَمِ

32. His constraint through poverty only
confirmed his detachment from them.
A need such as his shall not lead to transgression.

Purity and poverty,
    the prayers of your heart;
Strong-heartedness and chivalry,
    a hero but apart.
ANON.

48

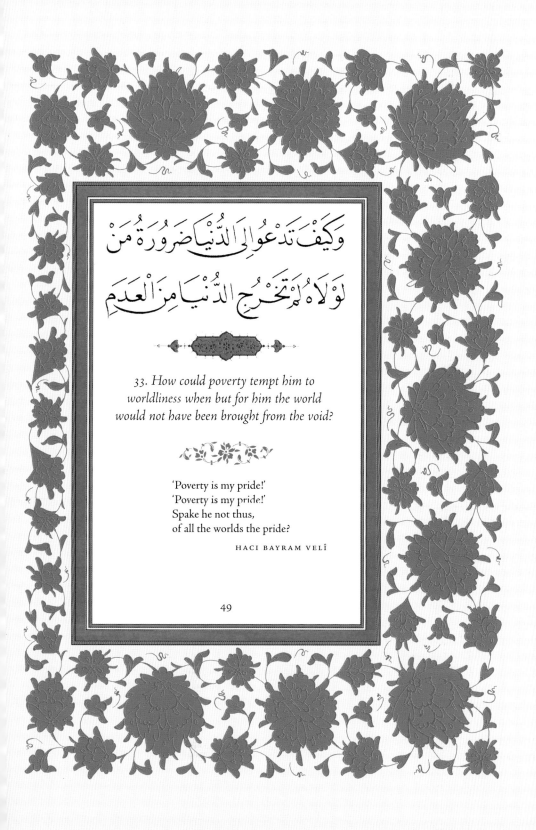

وَكَيْفَ تَدْعُوإِلَى الدُّنْيَا ضَرُورَةُ مَنْ
لَوْلَاهُ لَمْ تَخْرُجِ الدُّنْيَا مِنَ الْعَدَمِ

33. *How could poverty tempt him to*
worldliness when but for him the world
would not have been brought from the void?

'Poverty is my pride!'
'Poverty is my pride!'
Spake he not thus,
of all the worlds the pride?

HACI BAYRAM VELÎ

49

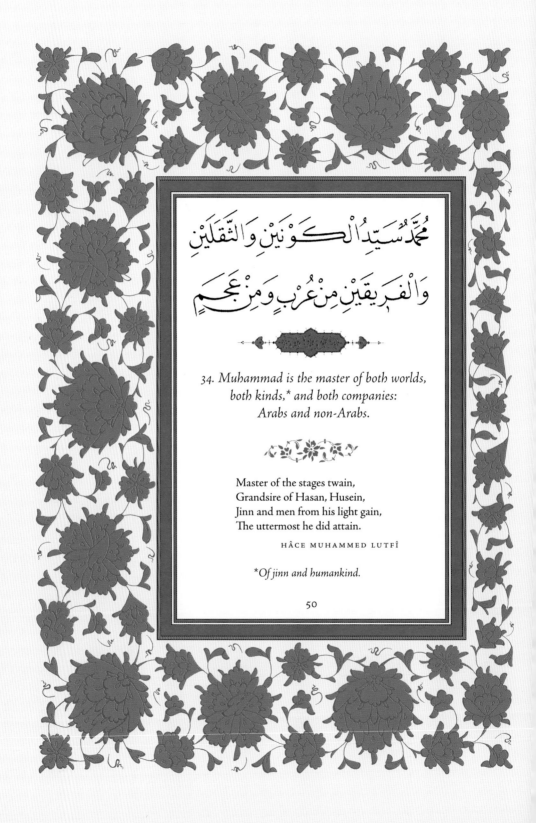

مُحَمَّدٌ سَيِّدُ الْكَوْنَيْنِ وَالثَّقَلَيْنِ

وَالْفَرِيقَيْنِ مِنْ عُرْبٍ وَمِنْ عَجَمِ

34. Muhammad is the master of both worlds,
both kinds,* and both companies:
Arabs and non-Arabs.

Master of the stages twain,
Grandsire of Hasan, Husein,
Jinn and men from his light gain,
The uttermost he did attain.

HÂCE MUHAMMED LUTFÎ

*Of jinn and humankind.

50

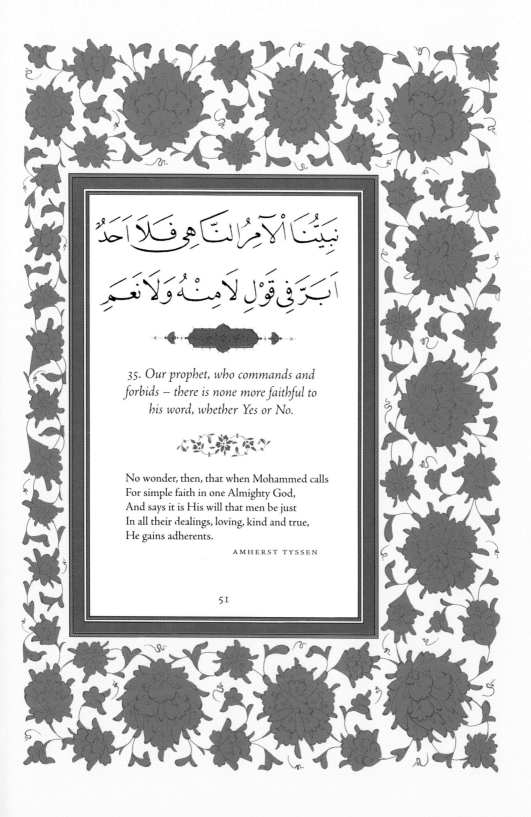

نَبِيِّنَا الْآمِرُ النَّاهِى فَلَا أَحَدُ
أَبَرَّ فِى قَوْلٍ لَا مِنْهُ وَلَا نَعَمْ

35. *Our prophet, who commands and
forbids – there is none more faithful to
his word, whether Yes or No.*

No wonder, then, that when Mohammed calls
For simple faith in one Almighty God,
And says it is His will that men be just
In all their dealings, loving, kind and true,
He gains adherents.

AMHERST TYSSEN

51

هُوَ الْحَبِيبُ الَّذِى تُرْجَى شَفَاعَتُهُ

لِكُلِّ هَوْلٍ مِنَ الْأَهْوَالِ مُقْتَحِمِ

36. *He is the loved one whose intercession*
is hoped for; a victor against every terror
and calamity.

He it is who intercedes
in this world and the next!
He it is whose plea exceeds
the ken of men perplexed!

RUMI

52

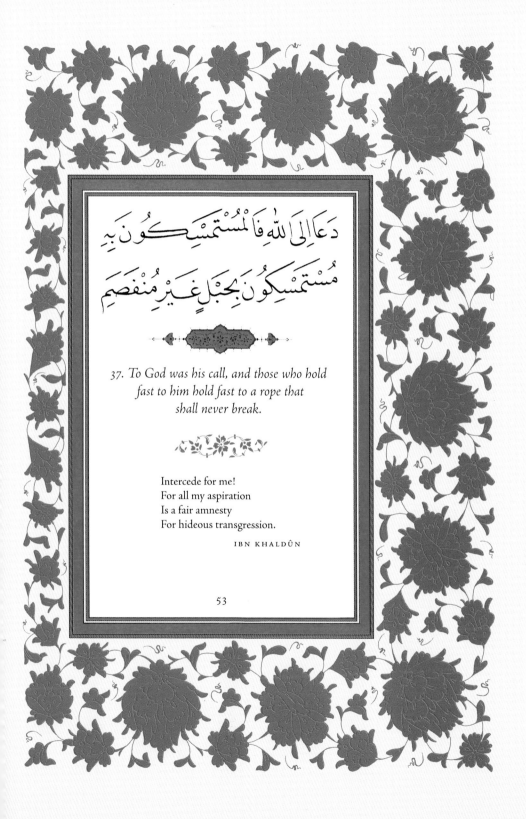

دَعَا إِلَى اللهِ فَالْمُسْتَمْسِكُونَ بِهِ

مُسْتَمْسِكُونَ بِحَبْلٍ غَيْرِ مُنْفَصِمِ

37. *To God was his call, and those who hold*
fast to him hold fast to a rope that
shall never break.

Intercede for me!
For all my aspiration
Is a fair amnesty
For hideous transgression.

IBN KHALDÛN

53

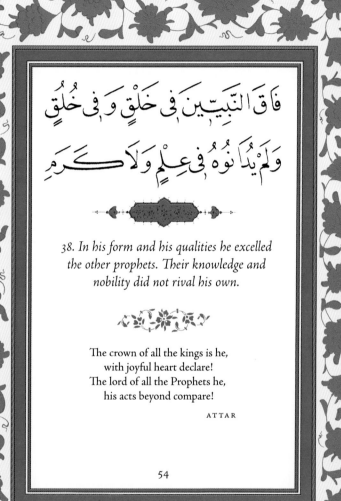

فَاقَ النَّبِيِّينَ فِى خَلْقٍ وَ فِى خُلُقٍ
وَلَمْ يُدَانُوهُ فِى عِلْمٍ وَلَا كَرَمِ

38. *In his form and his qualities he excelled*
the other prophets. Their knowledge and
nobility did not rival his own.

The crown of all the kings is he,
with joyful heart declare!
The lord of all the Prophets he,
his acts beyond compare!

ATTAR

54

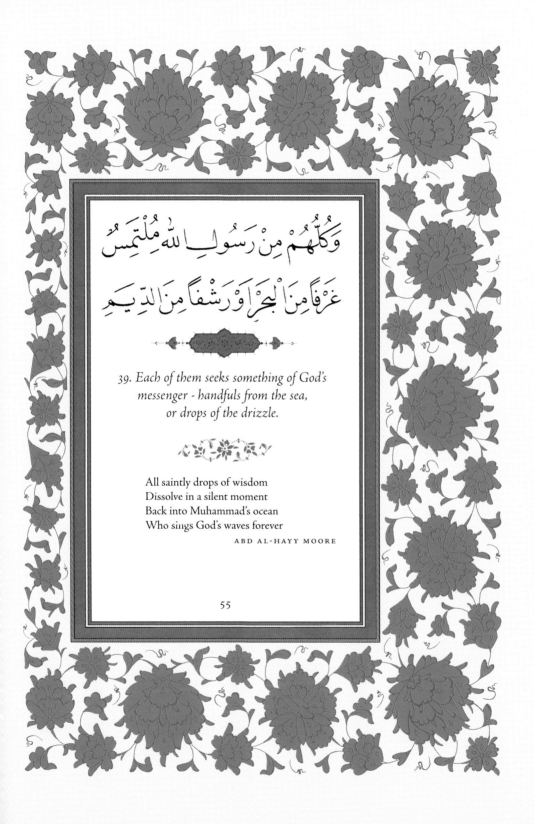

وَكُلُّهُمْ مِنْ رَسُولِ اللهِ مُلْتَمِسٌ

غَرْفًا مِنَ الْبَحْرِ أَوْ رَشْفًا مِنَ الدِّيَمِ

39. *Each of them seeks something of God's*
messenger - handfuls from the sea,
or drops of the drizzle.

All saintly drops of wisdom
Dissolve in a silent moment
Back into Muhammad's ocean
Who sings God's waves forever

ABD AL-HAYY MOORE

55

وَوَاقِفُونَ لَدَيْهِ عِنْدَ حَدِّهِمْ

مِنْ نُقْطَةِ الْعِلْمِ أَوْ مِنْ شَكْلَةِ الْحِكَمِ

40. *Before him do they stand, respecting*
their limits; dots to his knowledge,
or vowel-signs to his wisdom.

An earthly being flew
Unto the Throne of God.
Unlettered yet he knew.
His heart a library was.

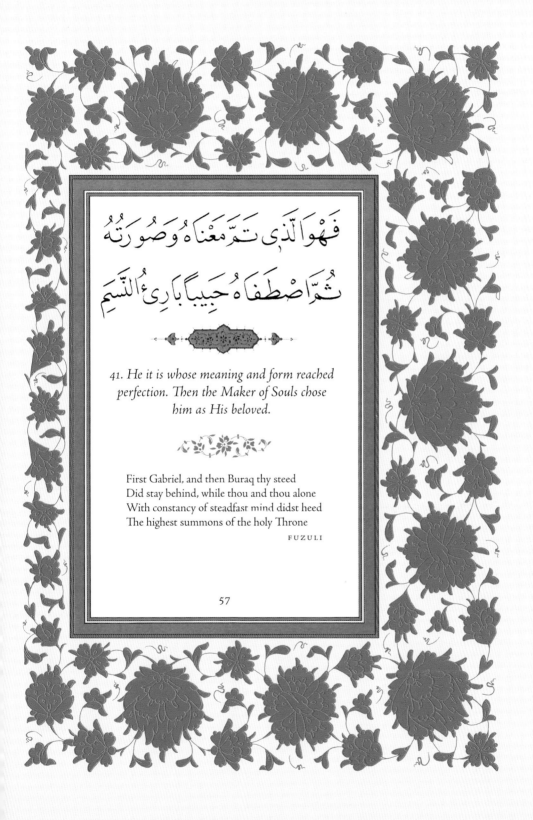

فَهُوَ ٱلَّذِى تَمَّ مَعْنَاهُ وَصُورَتُهُ

ثُمَّ ٱصْطَفَاهُ حَبِيبًا بَارِئُ ٱلنَّسَمِ

41. He it is whose meaning and form reached
perfection. Then the Maker of Souls chose
him as His beloved.

First Gabriel, and then Buraq thy steed
Did stay behind, while thou and thou alone
With constancy of steadfast mind didst heed
The highest summons of the holy Throne

FUZULI

57

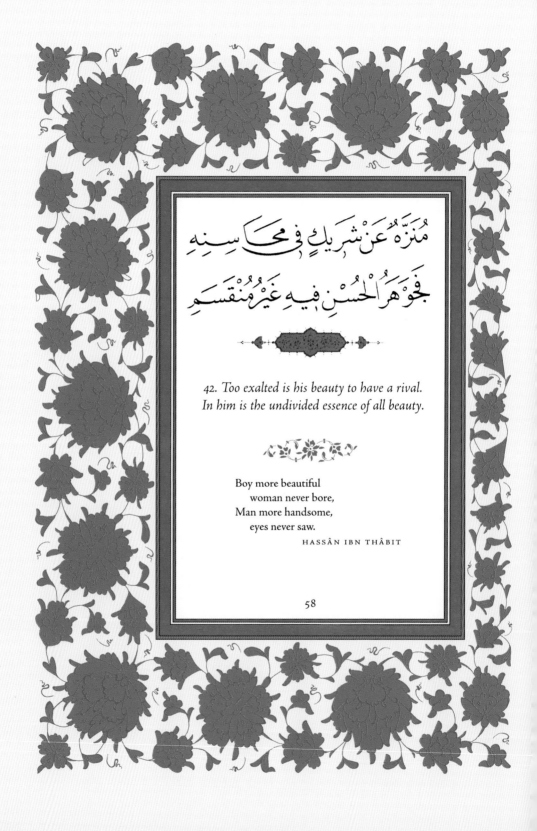

مُنزَّهٌ عَنْ شَرِيكٍ فِى مَحَاسِنِهِ

فَجَوْهَرُ الْحُسْنِ فِيهِ غَيْرُ مُنْقَسِمِ

42. *Too exalted is his beauty to have a rival.*
In him is the undivided essence of all beauty.

Boy more beautiful
   woman never bore,
Man more handsome,
   eyes never saw.

HASSÂN IBN THÂBIT

58

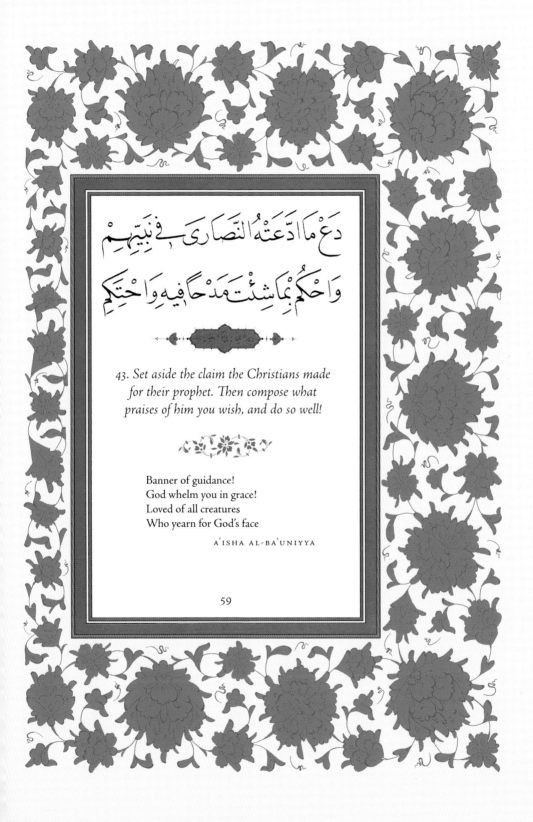

دَعْ مَا ادَّعَتْهُ النَّصَارَى فِي نَبِيِّهِمْ

وَاحْكُمْ بِمَا شِئْتَ مَدْحًا فِيهِ وَاحْتَكِمِ

43. *Set aside the claim the Christians made*
for their prophet. Then compose what
praises of him you wish, and do so well!

Banner of guidance!
God whelm you in grace!
Loved of all creatures
Who yearn for God's face

A'ISHA AL-BA'UNIYYA

59

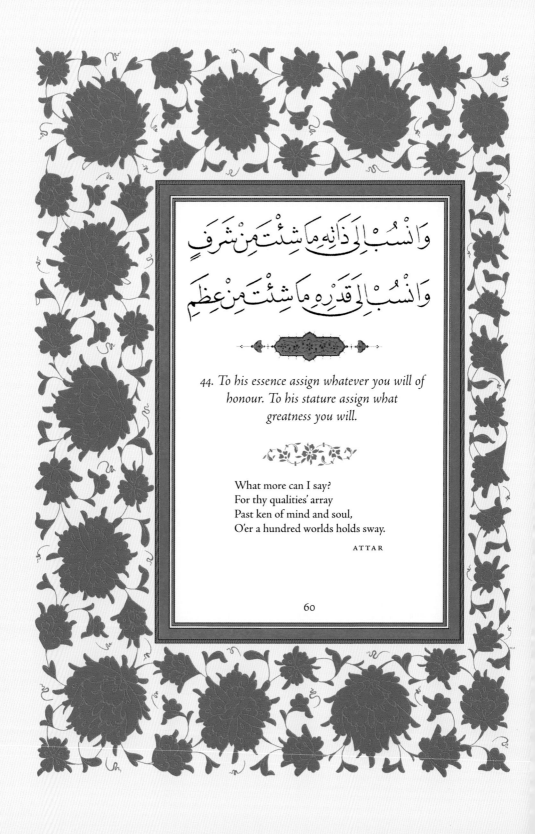

وَانْسُبْ اِلَى ذَاتِهِ مَا شِئْتَ مِنْ شَرَفٍ

وَانْسُبْ اِلَى قَدْرِهِ مَا شِئْتَ مِنْ عِظَمِ

44. *To his essence assign whatever you will of
honour. To his stature assign what
greatness you will.*

What more can I say?
For thy qualities' array
Past ken of mind and soul,
O'er a hundred worlds holds sway.

ATTAR

60

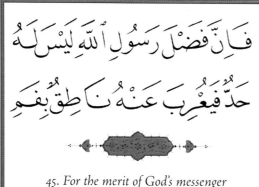

فَاِنَّ فَضْلَ رَسُولِ ٱللَّهِ لَيْسَ لَهُ
حَدَّ فَيُعْرِبُ عَنْهُ نَاطِقٌ بِفَمِ

45. For the merit of God's messenger
knows no bounds that might be voiced by the
mouths of men.

Why do I talk so long? I fail to see
A limit to my theme's fertility.

FIRDAWSI

61

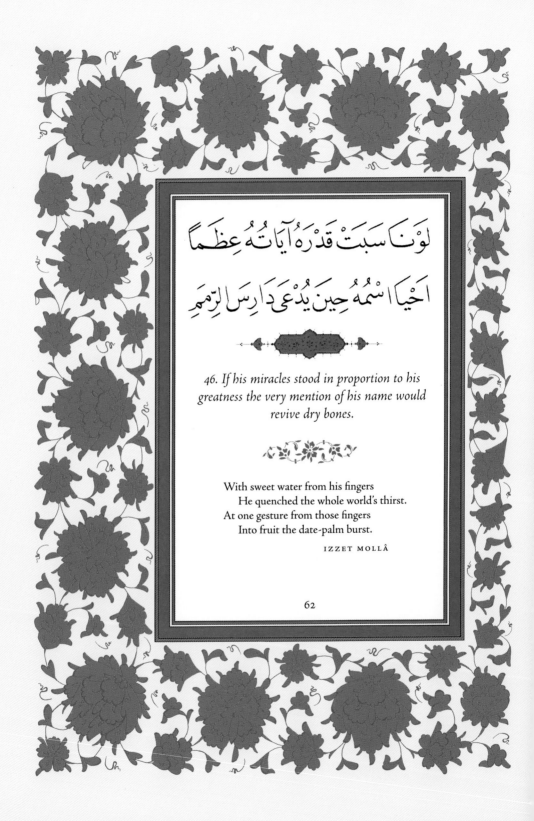

لَوْ نَاسَبَتْ قَدْرَهُ آيَاتُهُ عِظَمًا

اَحْيَا اسْمُهُ حِينَ يُدْعَى دَارِسَ الرَّمَمِ

46. *If his miracles stood in proportion to his*
greatness the very mention of his name would
revive dry bones.

With sweet water from his fingers
    He quenched the whole world's thirst.
At one gesture from those fingers
    Into fruit the date-palm burst.

IZZET MOLLÂ

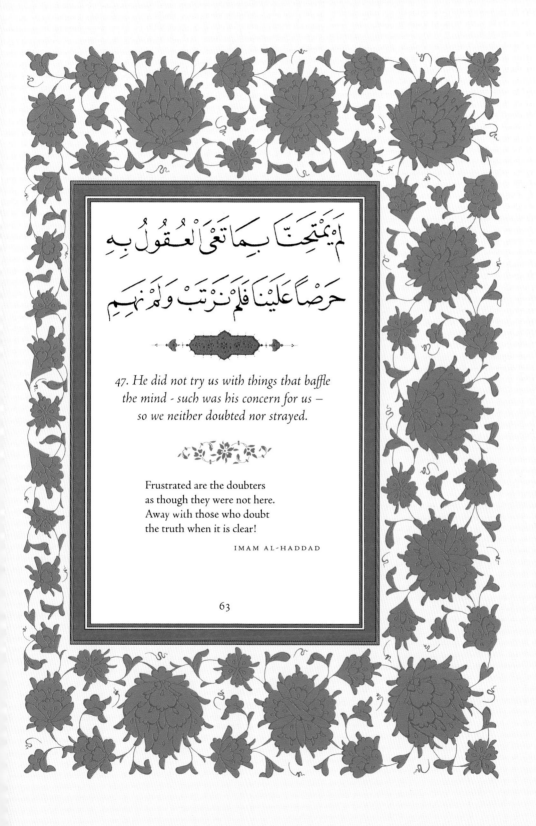

لَمْ يَمْتَحِنَّا بِمَا تَعْيَى الْعُقُولُ بِهِ

حِرْصًا عَلَيْنَا فَلَمْ نَرْتَبْ وَلَمْ نَهِمِ

47. *He did not try us with things that baffle*
the mind - such was his concern for us –
so we neither doubted nor strayed.

Frustrated are the doubters
as though they were not here.
Away with those who doubt
the truth when it is clear!

IMAM AL-HADDAD

63

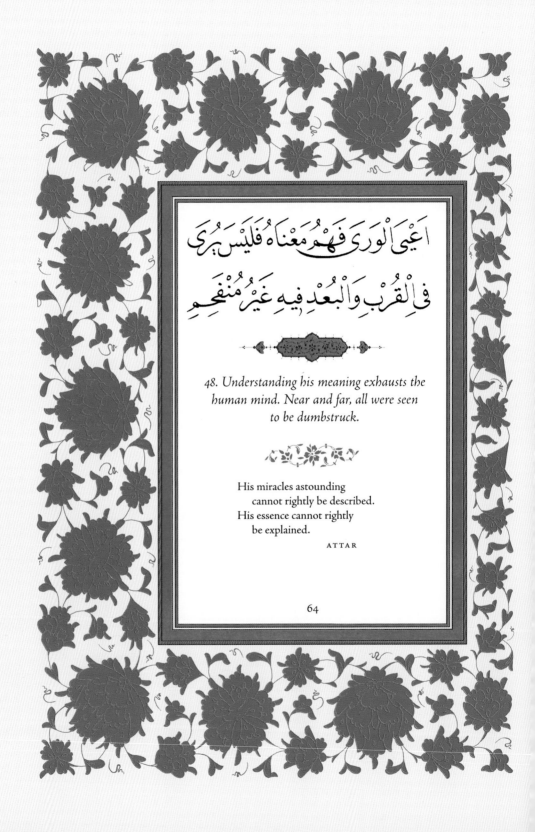

اَعْيَا الْوَرَى فَهُمُ مَعْنَاهُ فَلَيْسَ يُرَى فِى الْقُرْبِ وَالْبُعْدِ فِيهِ غَيْرُ مُنْفَحِمٍ

48. *Understanding his meaning exhausts the*
human mind. Near and far, all were seen
to be dumbstruck.

His miracles astounding
cannot rightly be described.
His essence cannot rightly
be explained.

ATTAR

64

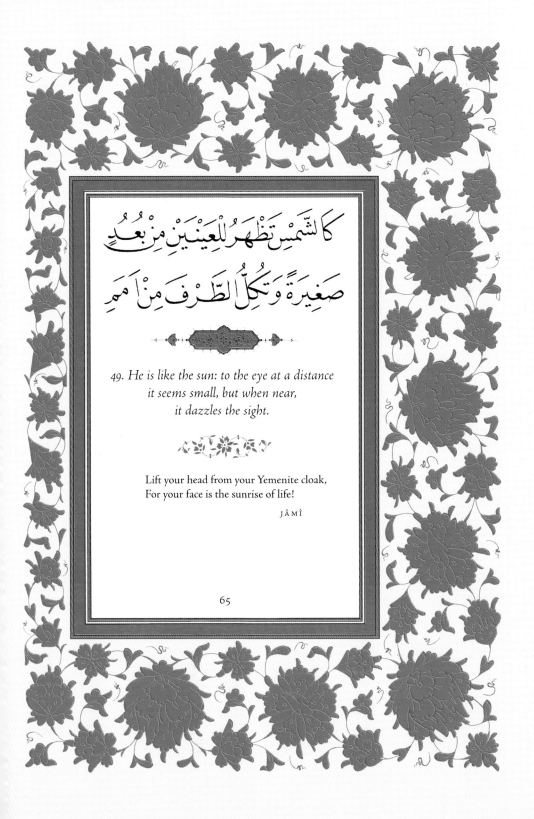

كَالشَّمْسِ تَظْهَرُ لِلْعَيْنَيْنِ مِنْ بُعُدٍ

صَغِيرَةً وَتُكِلُّ الطَّرْفَ مِنْ أَمَمِ

49. He is like the sun: to the eye at a distance
it seems small, but when near,
it dazzles the sight.

Lift your head from your Yemenite cloak,
For your face is the sunrise of life!

JÂMÎ

65

وَكَيْفَ يُدْرِكُ فِى الدُّنْيَا حَقِيقَتَهُ

قَوْمٌ نِيَامٌ تَسَلَّوْا عَنْهُ بِالْحُلُمِ

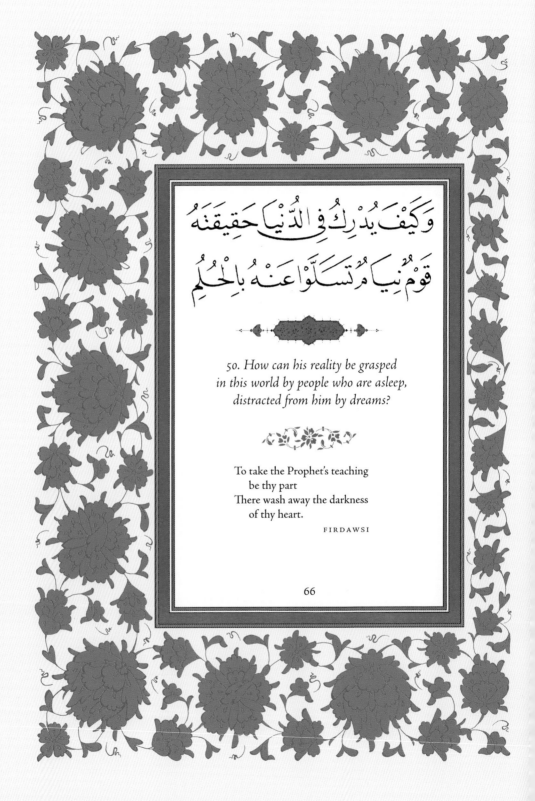

50. How can his reality be grasped
in this world by people who are asleep,
distracted from him by dreams?

To take the Prophet's teaching
be thy part
There wash away the darkness
of thy heart.

FIRDAWSI

66

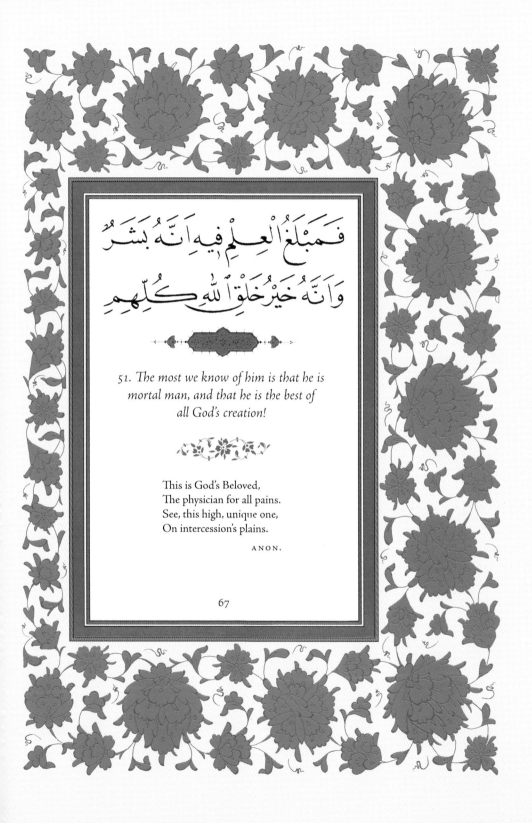

فَمَبْلَغُ الْعِلْمِ فِيهِ اَنَّهُ بَشَرُ
وَاَنَّهُ خَيْرُ خَلْقِ اللهِ كُلِّهِمِ

51. *The most we know of him is that he is*
mortal man, and that he is the best of
all God's creation!

This is God's Beloved,
The physician for all pains.
See, this high, unique one,
On intercession's plains.

ANON.

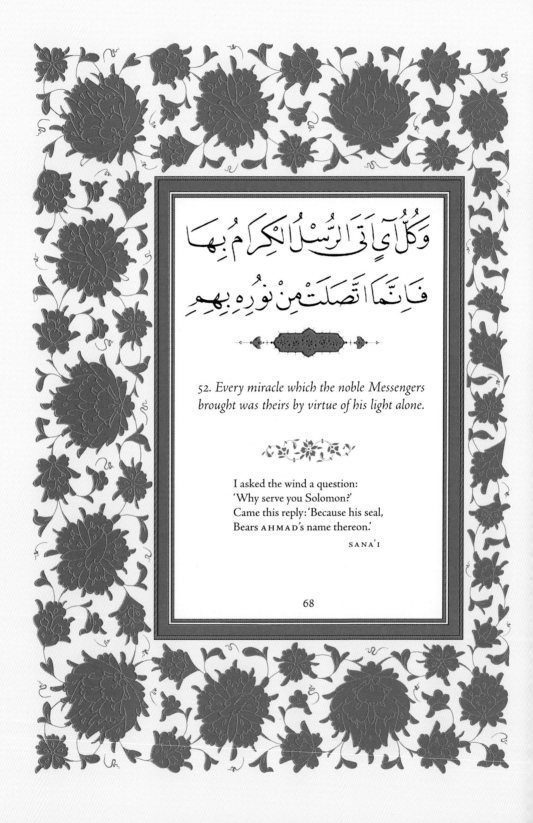

وَكُلُّ آيٍ آتَى الرُّسُلُ الْكِرَامُ بِهَا
فَإِنَّمَا اتَّصَلَتْ مِنْ نُورِهِ بِهِمْ

52. *Every miracle which the noble Messengers*
brought was theirs by virtue of his light alone.

I asked the wind a question:
'Why serve you Solomon?'
Came this reply: 'Because his seal,
Bears AHMAD's name thereon.'

SANA'I

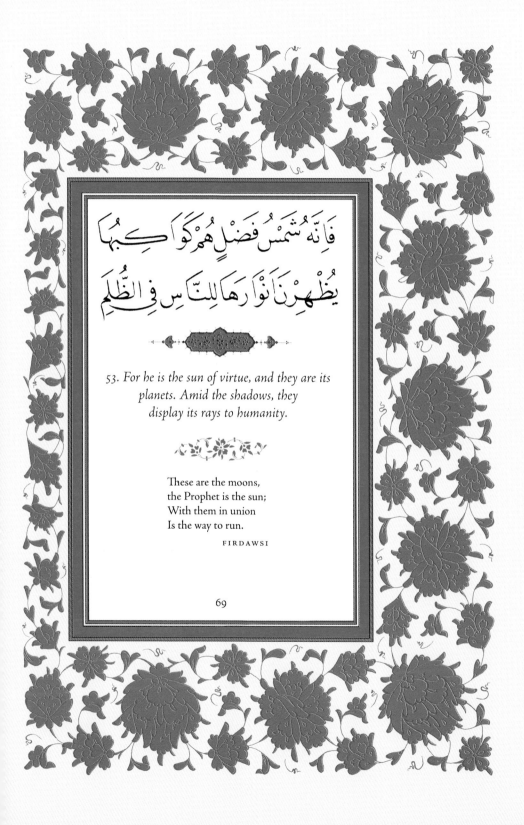

فَإِنَّهُ شَمْسُ فَضْلٍ هُمْ كَوَا كِبُهَا

يُظْهِرْنَ أَنْوَارَهَا لِلنَّاسِ فِى الظُّلَمِ

53. For he is the sun of virtue, and they are its
planets. Amid the shadows, they
display its rays to humanity.

These are the moons,
the Prophet is the sun;
With them in union
Is the way to run.

FIRDAWSI

69

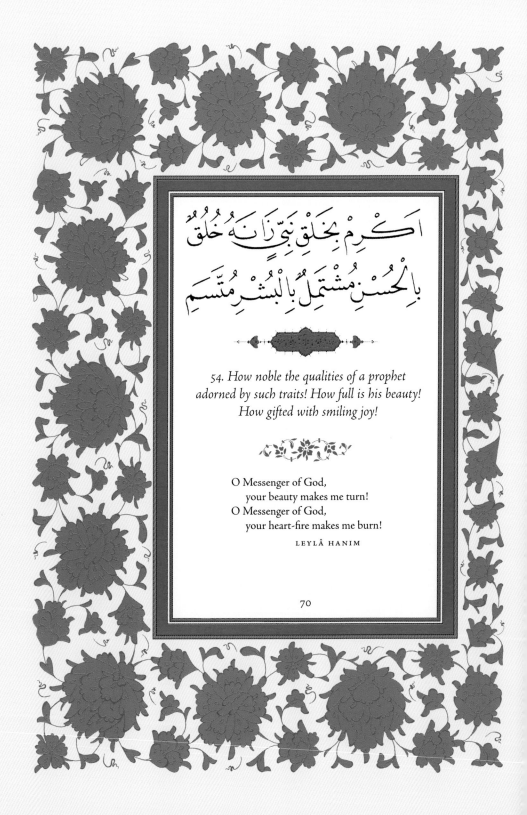

اَكْرِمْ بِخَلْقٍ نَبِيٍّ زَانَهُ خُلُقٌ
بِالْحُسْنِ مُشْتَمِلٌ بِالْبِشْرِ مُتَّسِمِ

54. How noble the qualities of a prophet
adorned by such traits! How full is his beauty!
How gifted with smiling joy!

O Messenger of God,
    your beauty makes me turn!
O Messenger of God,
    your heart-fire makes me burn!

LEYLÂ HANIM

70

كَالزَّهْرِ فِي تَرَفٍ وَالْبَدْرِ فِي شَرَفٍ

وَالْبَحْرِ فِي كَرَمٍ وَالدَّهْرِ فِي هِمَمِ

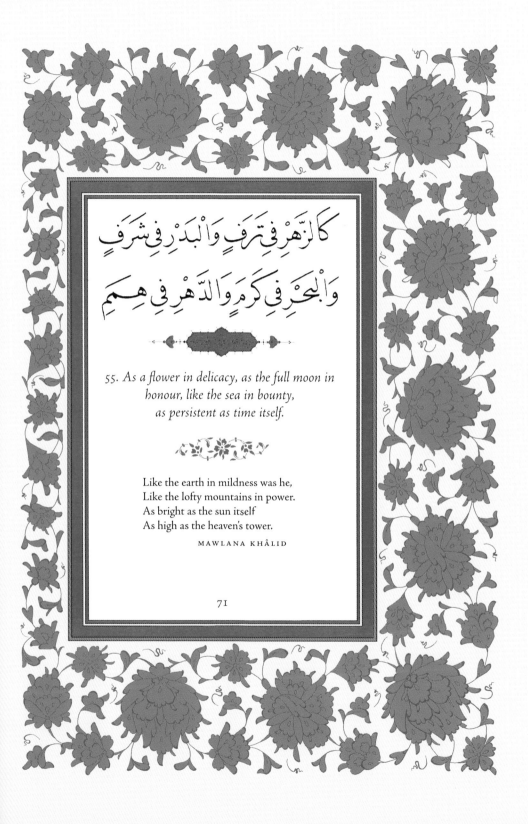

55. *As a flower in delicacy, as the full moon in*
honour, like the sea in bounty,
as persistent as time itself.

Like the earth in mildness was he,
Like the lofty mountains in power.
As bright as the sun itself
As high as the heaven's tower.

MAWLANA KHÂLID

71

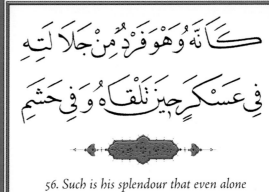

كَانَهُ وَهُوَ فَرْدٌ مِنْ جَلَالَتِهِ

فِي عَسْكَرٍ حِينَ تَلْقَاهُ وَفِي حَشَمِ

56. Such is his splendour that even alone
in his glory superb courtiers and guards
seem to stand around him.

Where all is private,
thou alone wert found,
Where none attained,
attainment thou didst find.

72

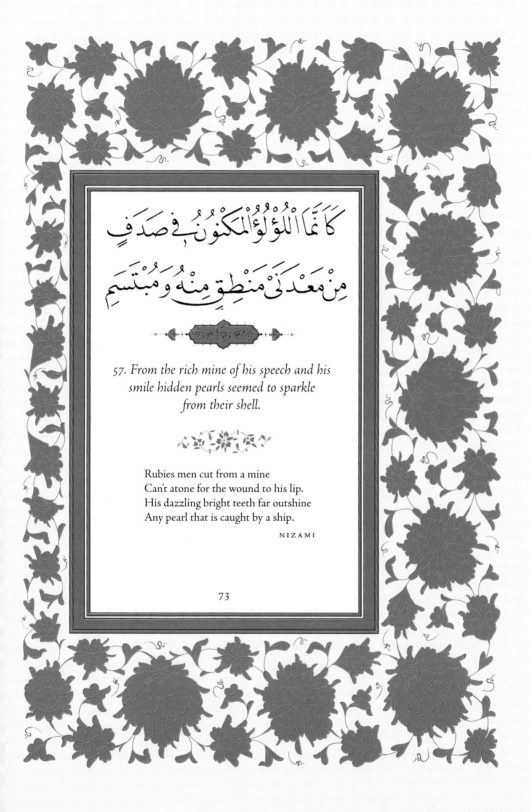

كَأَنَّمَا اللُّؤْلُؤُالْمَكْنُونُ فِي صَدَفٍ

مِنْ مَعْدَنَىْ مَنْطِقٍ مِنْهُ وَمُبْتَسِمِ

57. From the rich mine of his speech and his
smile hidden pearls seemed to sparkle
from their shell.

Rubies men cut from a mine
Can't atone for the wound to his lip.
His dazzling bright teeth far outshine
Any pearl that is caught by a ship.

NIZAMI

73

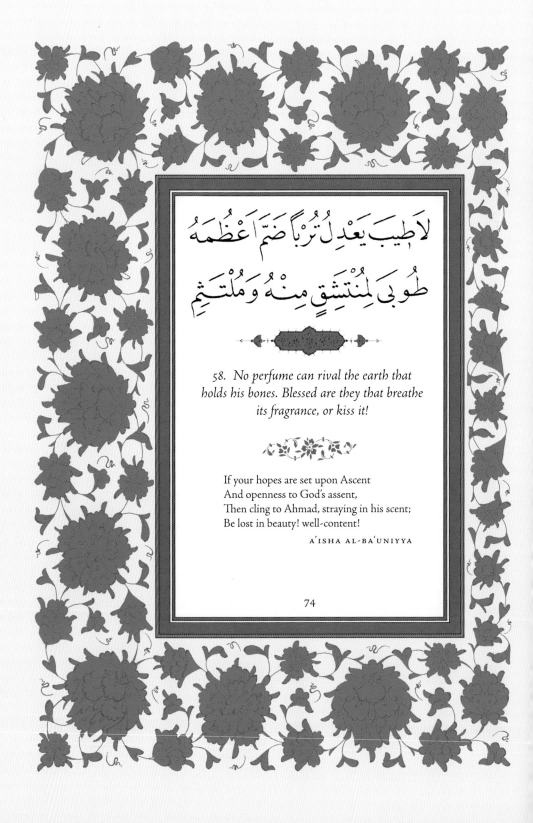

لَا طِيبَ يَعْدِلُ تُرْباً ضَمَّ اَعْظُمَهُ

طُوبَى لِمُنْتَشِقٍ مِنْهُ وَمُلْتَثِمِ

58. *No perfume can rival the earth that*
holds his bones. Blessed are they that breathe
its fragrance, or kiss it!

If your hopes are set upon Ascent
And openness to God's assent,
Then cling to Ahmad, straying in his scent;
Be lost in beauty! well-content!

A'ISHA AL-BA'UNIYYA

74

ابَاَنَ مَوْلِدُهُ عَنْ طِيبِ عُنْصُرِهِ
يَا طِيبَ مُبْتَدَأٍ مِنْهُ وَمُخْتَتَمِ

*59. His birth revealed the purity of his ancestry.
How fine his origin, how pure
his final end!*

Lady Amine,
   Muhammed's mother she,
(From this Shell
   yon Pearl did come to be.)
SÜLEYMAN ÇELEBI

75

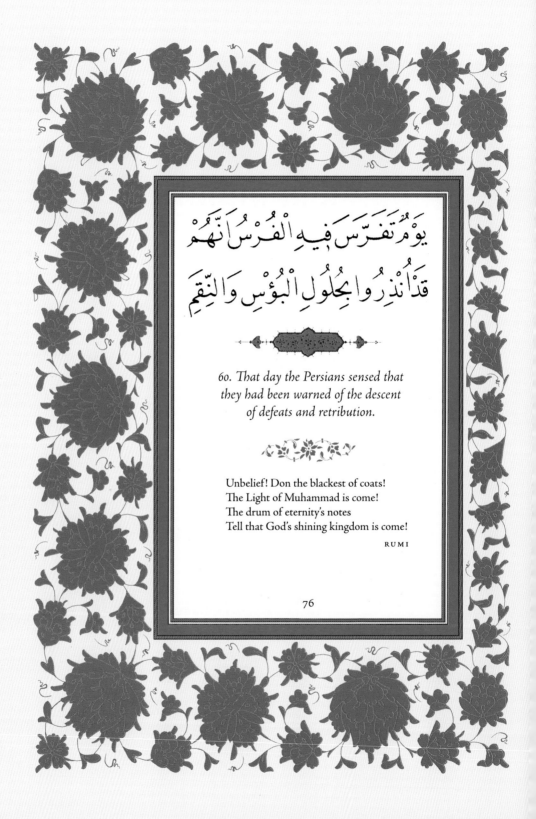

يَوْمُ تَفَرَّسَ فِيهِ الْفُرْسُ اَنَّهُمْ

قَدْ اُنْذِرُوا بِحُلُولِ الْبُؤْسِ وَالنِّقَمْ

60. *That day the Persians sensed that*
they had been warned of the descent
of defeats and retribution.

Unbelief! Don the blackest of coats!
The Light of Muhammad is come!
The drum of eternity's notes
Tell that God's shining kingdom is come!

RUMI

76

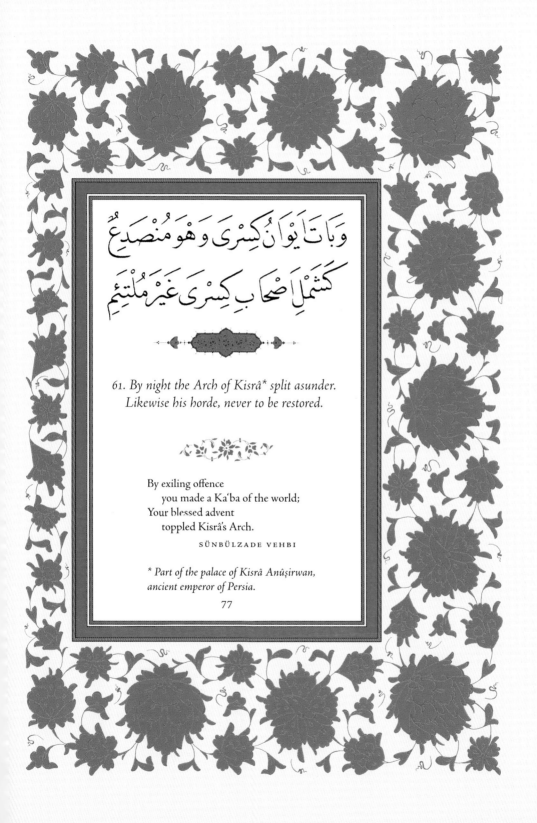

وَبَاتَ ايْوَانُ كِسْرَى وَهُوَ مُنْصَدِعٌ
كَشَمْلِ اَصْحَابِ كِسْرَى غَيْرَ مُلْتَئِمِ

61. *By night the Arch of Kisrâ* split asunder.*
Likewise his horde, never to be restored.

By exiling offence
    you made a Ka'ba of the world;
Your blessed advent
    toppled Kisrâ's Arch.

SÜNBÜLZADE VEHBI

* *Part of the palace of Kisrâ Anûṣirwan,*
ancient emperor of Persia.

77

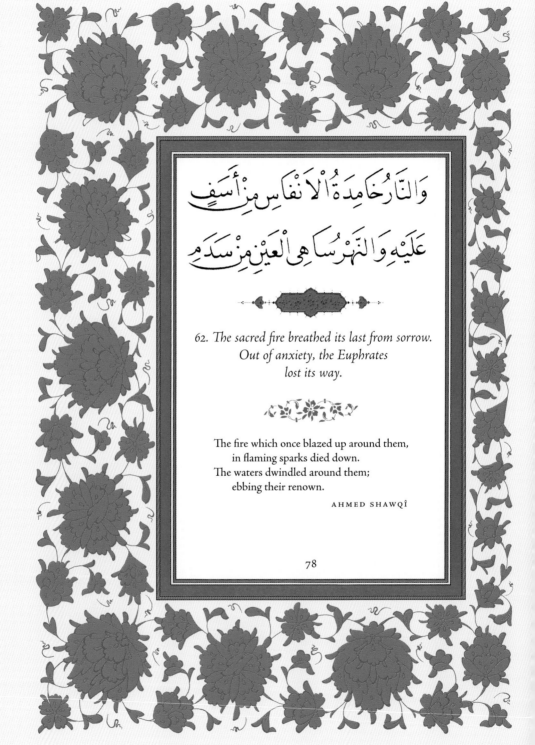

وَالنَّارُ خَامِدَةُ الْأَنْفَاسِ مِنْ أَسَفٍ

عَلَيْهِ وَالنَّهْرُ سَاهِى الْعَيْنِ مِنْ سَدَمٍ

62. The sacred fire breathed its last from sorrow.
Out of anxiety, the Euphrates
lost its way.

The fire which once blazed up around them,
in flaming sparks died down.
The waters dwindled around them;
ebbing their renown.

AHMED SHAWQÎ

78

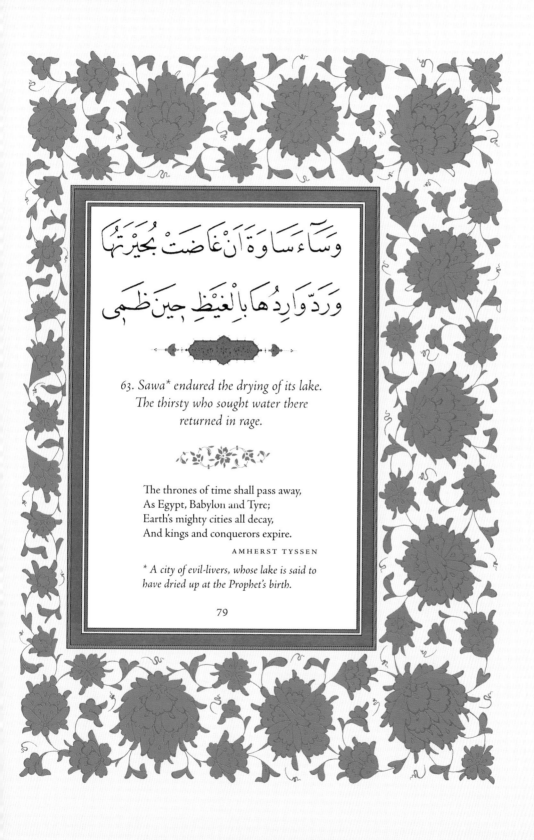

وَسَاءَ سَاوَةَ أَنْ غَاضَتْ بُحَيْرَتُهَا

وَرَدَّ وَارِدُهَا بِالْغَيْظِ حِينَ ظَمِى

63. Sawa* endured the drying of its lake.
The thirsty who sought water there
returned in rage.

The thrones of time shall pass away,
As Egypt, Babylon and Tyre;
Earth's mighty cities all decay,
And kings and conquerors expire.

AMHERST TYSSEN

* A city of evil-livers, whose lake is said to
have dried up at the Prophet's birth.

79

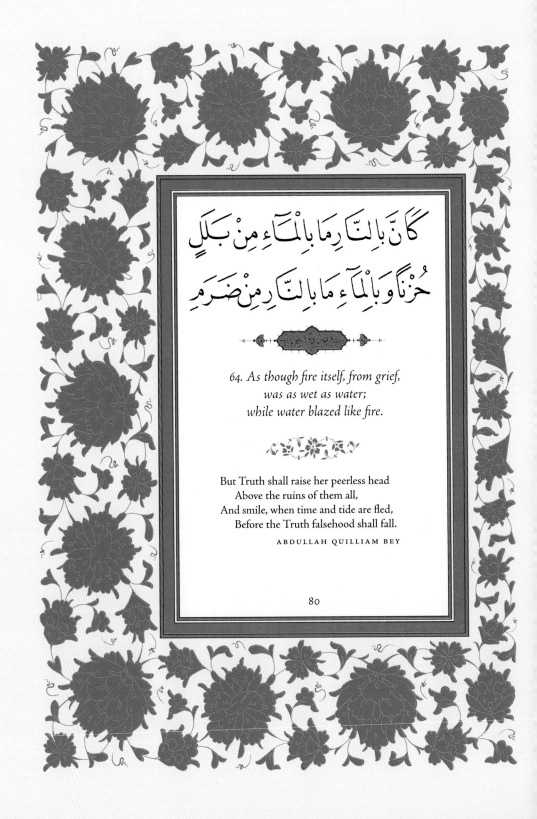

كَانَ بِالنَّارِ مَا بِالْمَاءِ مِنْ بَلَلٍ

حُزْنًا وَبِالْمَاءِ مَا بِالنَّارِ مِنْ ضَرَمٍ

64. *As though fire itself, from grief,*
was as wet as water;
while water blazed like fire.

But Truth shall raise her peerless head
Above the ruins of them all,
And smile, when time and tide are fled,
Before the Truth falsehood shall fall.

ABDULLAH QUILLIAM BEY

80

وَالْجِنُّ تَهْتِفُ وَالْأَنْوَارُ سَاطِعَةٌ
وَالْحَقُّ يَظْهَرُ مِنْ مَعْنًى وَمِنْ كَلِمٍ

65. Jinn called out. Lights shone, dazzling.
Truth was made manifest
in word and in fact.

You led the wanderer back to Truth's fair road,
And held the hand of succour to the lost,
On all the world you counselling bestowed,
The field of every action you have crossed.

FUZULI

81

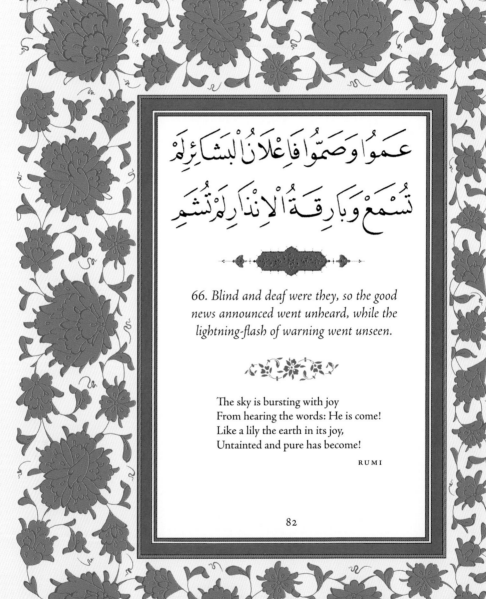

عَمُوا وَصَمُّوا فَاعْلانُ الْبَشَائِرَلَمْ
تُسْمَعْ وَبارِقَةُ الْاِنْذارِلَمْ تُشَمِ

66. *Blind and deaf were they, so the good*
news announced went unheard, while the
lightning-flash of warning went unseen.

The sky is bursting with joy
From hearing the words: He is come!
Like a lily the earth in its joy,
Untainted and pure has become!

RUMI

82

مِنْ بَعْدِ مَا أَخْبَرَالْأَقْوَامَ كَاهِنُهُمْ

بِانَّ دِينَهُمُ الْمُعَوَّجَ لَمْ يَقُمِ

67. *This even though the diviners had*
advised their people that their crooked religion
could no longer stand.

As long as thy name's fresh breeze
                        does not blow
Upon religion's soft garden,
The branches lie still, refusing to grow,
The roots will not thrill but will harden.

SANA'I

83

وَبَعْدَ مَا عَايَنُوْا فِى الْأُفُقِ مِنْ شُهُبٍ

مُنْقَضَّةٍ وَفُوْقَ مَا فِى الْأَرْضِ مِنْ صَنَمٍ

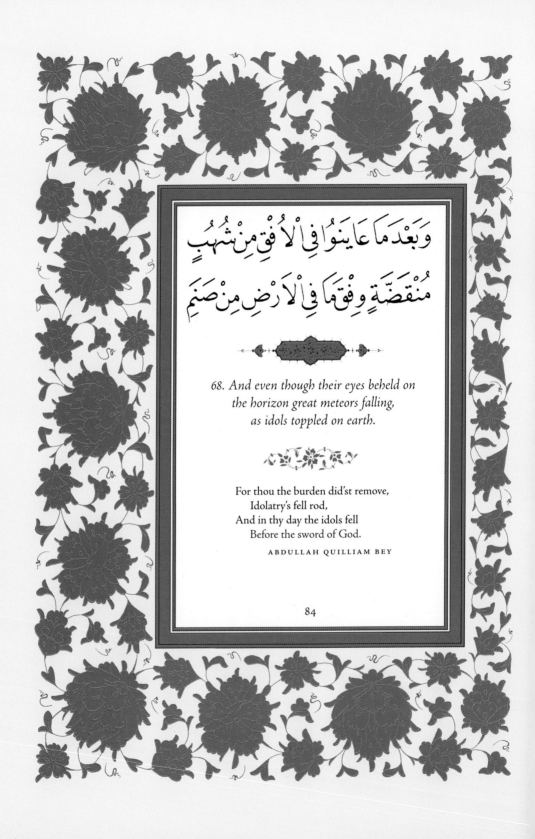

68. And even though their eyes beheld on
the horizon great meteors falling,
as idols toppled on earth.

For thou the burden did'st remove,
Idolatry's fell rod,
And in thy day the idols fell
Before the sword of God.

ABDULLAH QUILLIAM BEY

84

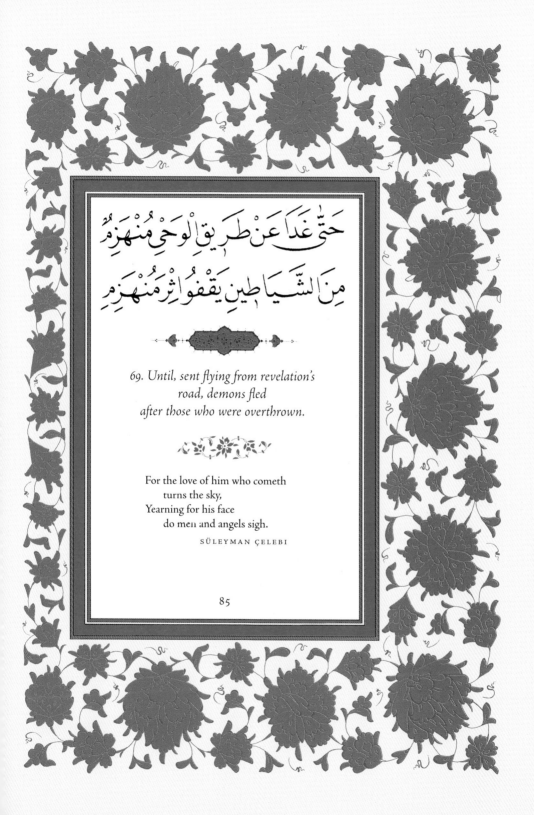

حَتَّى غَدَا عَنْ طَرِيقِ الْوَحْى مُنْهَزِمْ
مِنَ الشَّيَاطِينِ يَقْفُوا اثْرَ مُنْهَزِمْ

69. Until, sent flying from revelation's
road, demons fled
after those who were overthrown.

For the love of him who cometh
turns the sky,
Yearning for his face
do men and angels sigh.

SÜLEYMAN ÇELEBI

85

كَأَنَّهُمْ هَرَبًا أَبْطَالُ أَبْرَهَةِ

اوْ عَسْكَرٌ بِالْحَصَى مِنْ رَاحَتَيْهِ رُمِي

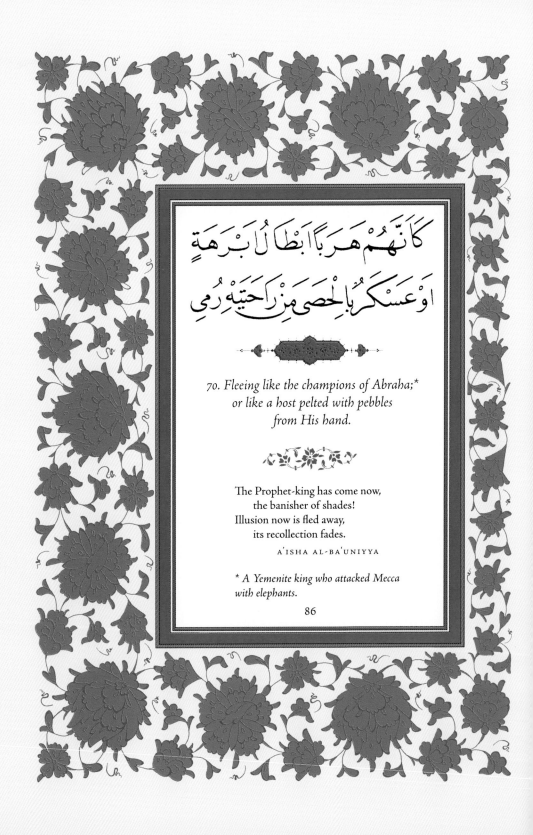

70. *Fleeing like the champions of Abraha;**
or like a host pelted with pebbles
from His hand.

The Prophet-king has come now,
the banisher of shades!
Illusion now is fled away,
its recollection fades.

A'ISHA AL-BA'UNIYYA

* A Yemenite king who attacked Mecca
with elephants.

86

نَبَذْنَا بِهِ بَعْدَ تَسْبِيحٍ بِبَطْنِهِمَا
نَبْذَ الْمُسَبِّحِ مِنْ أَحْشَاءِ مُلْتَقِمِ

71. *They sang glory in his hand, and then*
were cast like the praising Jonah,
cast from the whale's belly.

A fish, and then a sea,
With Jonah's praise within.
God uttered this decree:
Yield up what you drew in!

MAHMUT KAYA

87

جَاءَتْ لِدَعْوَتِهِ الْاَشْجَارُ سَاجِدَةً

تَمْشِى اِلَيْهِ عَلَى سَاقٍ بِلَا قَدَمِ

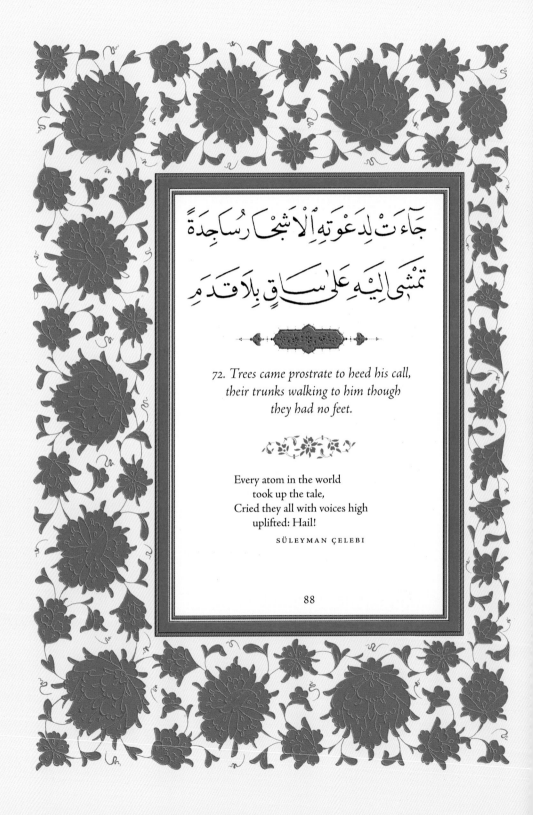

72. *Trees came prostrate to heed his call,*
their trunks walking to him though
they had no feet.

Every atom in the world
took up the tale,
Cried they all with voices high
uplifted: Hail!

SÜLEYMAN ÇELEBI

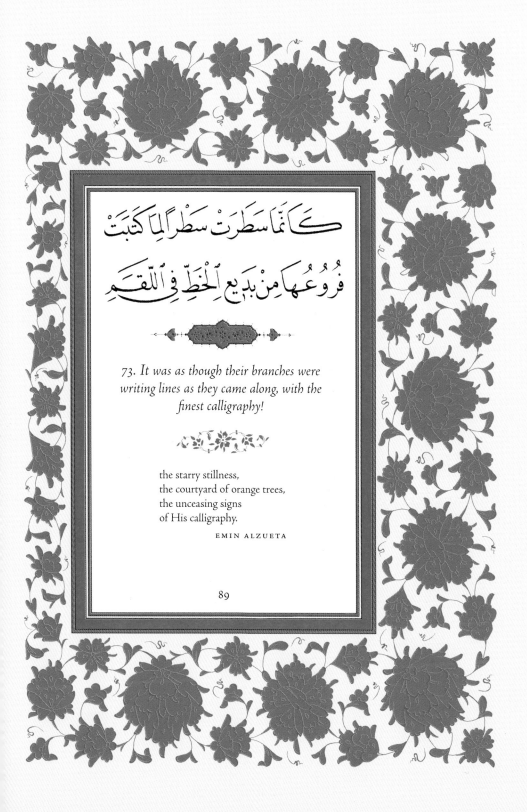

كَأَنَّمَا سَطَرَتْ سَطْرًا لِمَا كَتَبَتْ

فُرُوعُهَا مِنْ بَدِيعِ الْخَطِّ فِى اللَّقَمِ

73. *It was as though their branches were*
writing lines as they came along, with the
finest calligraphy!

the starry stillness,
the courtyard of orange trees,
the unceasing signs
of His calligraphy.

EMIN ALZUETA

89

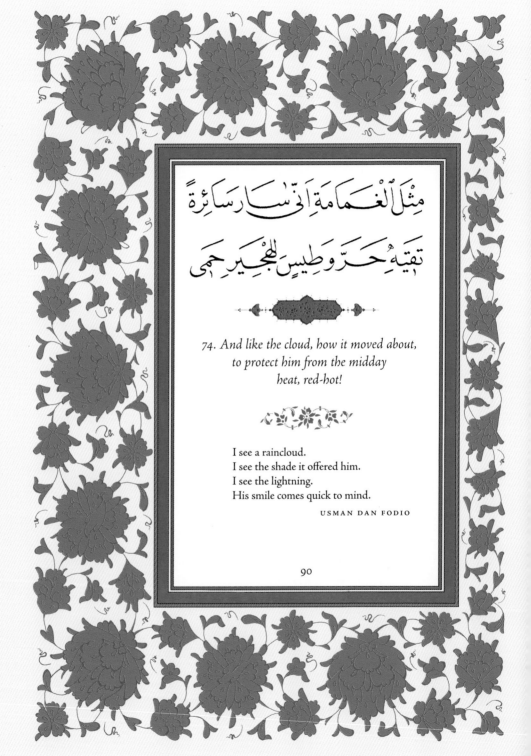

مِثْلَ الْغَمَامَةِ اَنَّى سَارَ سَائِرَةً

تَقِيهِ حَرَّ وَطِيسٍ الْهَجِيرِ حَمَى

74. And like the cloud, how it moved about,
to protect him from the midday
heat, red-hot!

I see a raincloud.
I see the shade it offered him.
I see the lightning.
His smile comes quick to mind.

USMAN DAN FODIO

90

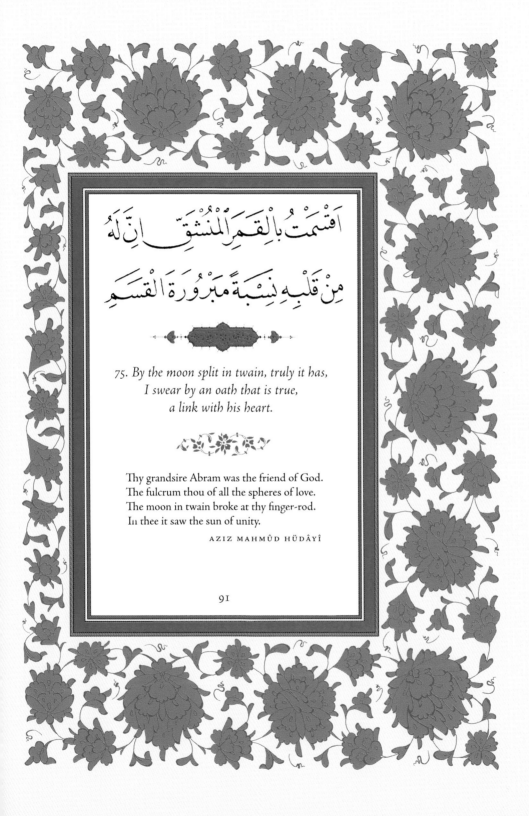

اَقْسَمْتُ بِالْقَمَرِ الْمُنْشَقِّ اِنَّ لَهُ

مِنْ قَلْبِهِ نِسْبَةً مَبْرُورَةَ الْقَسَمِ

75. *By the moon split in twain, truly it has,*
I swear by an oath that is true,
a link with his heart.

Thy grandsire Abram was the friend of God.
The fulcrum thou of all the spheres of love.
The moon in twain broke at thy finger-rod.
In thee it saw the sun of unity.

AZIZ MAHMÛD HÜDÂYÎ

91

وَمَا حَوَى ٱلْغَارُ مِنْ خَيْرٍ وَمِنْ كَرَمٍ

وَكُلُّ طَرْفٍ مِنَ ٱلْكُفَّارِ عَنْهُ عَمِي

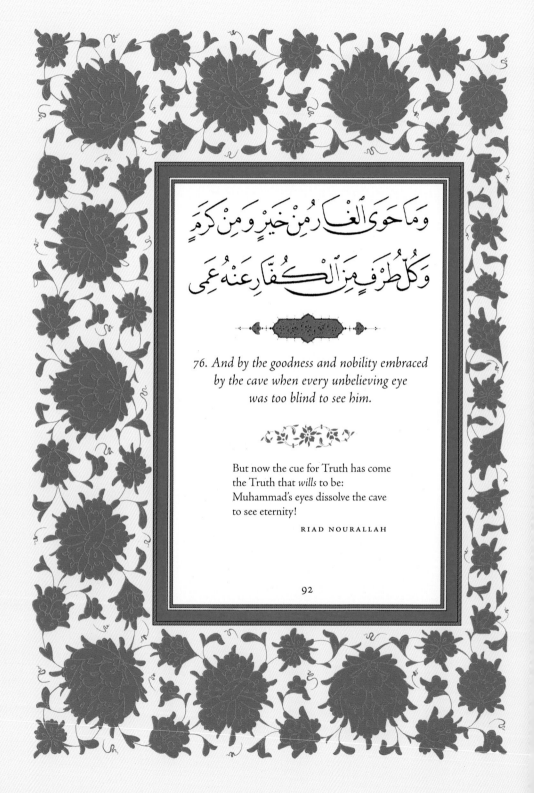

76. And by the goodness and nobility embraced
by the cave when every unbelieving eye
was too blind to see him.

But now the cue for Truth has come
the Truth that *wills* to be:
Muhammad's eyes dissolve the cave
to see eternity!

RIAD NOURALLAH

92

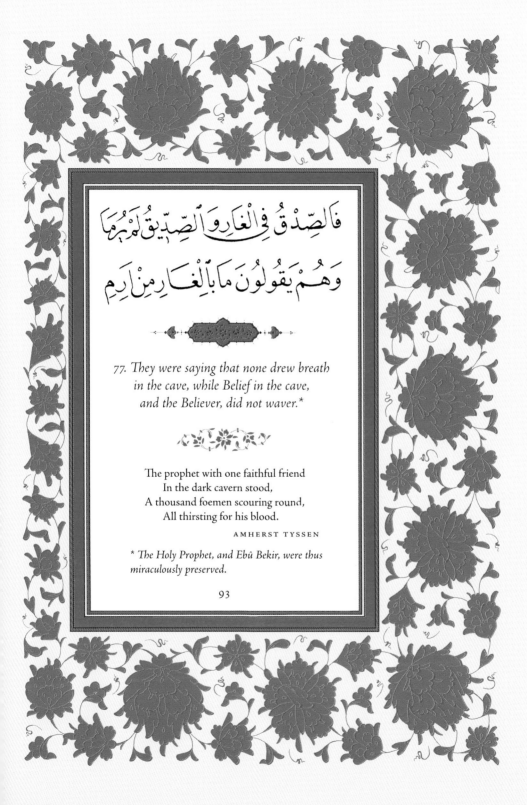

فَالصِّدْقُ فِى الْغَارِ وَالصِّدِّيقُ لَمْ يَرِمَا
وَهُمْ يَقُولُونَ مَا بِالْغَارِ مِنْ أَرِمِ

77. *They were saying that none drew breath*
in the cave, while Belief in the cave,
*and the Believer, did not waver.**

The prophet with one faithful friend
In the dark cavern stood,
A thousand foemen scouring round,
All thirsting for his blood.

AMHERST TYSSEN

* *The Holy Prophet, and Ebû Bekir, were thus*
miraculously preserved.

93

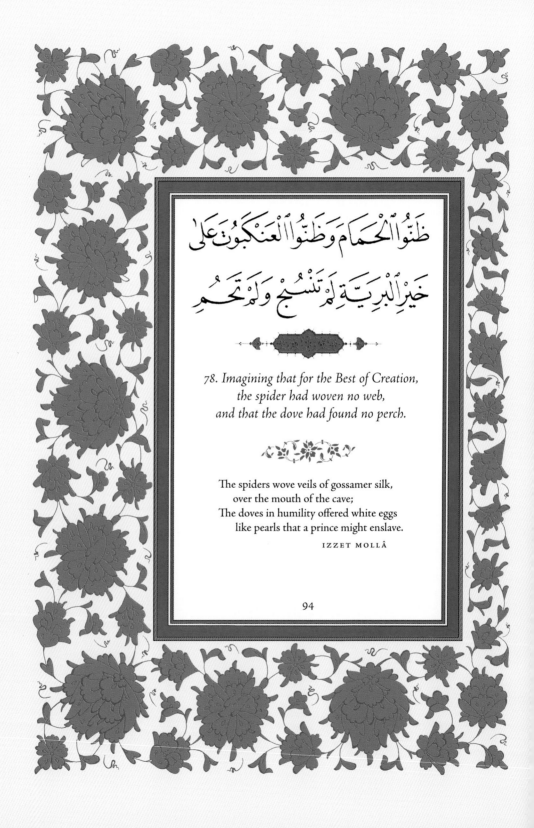

ظَنُّوا الْحَمَام وَظَنُّوا الْعَنْكَبُوتَ عَلَى

خَيْرِ الْبَرِيَّةِ لَمْ تَنْسُجْ وَلَمْ تَحِمِ

78. Imagining that for the Best of Creation,
the spider had woven no web,
and that the dove had found no perch.

The spiders wove veils of gossamer silk,
over the mouth of the cave;
The doves in humility offered white eggs
like pearls that a prince might enslave.

IZZET MOLLÂ

94

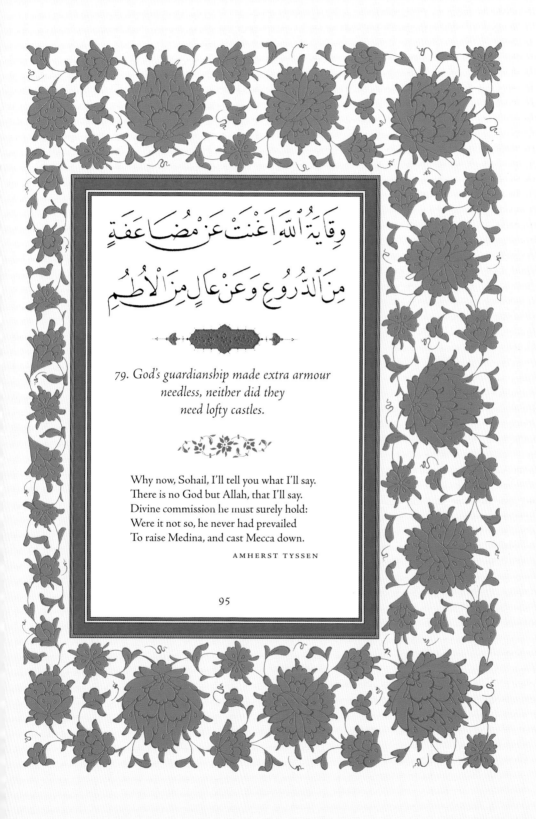

وِقَايَةُ اللهِ اغْنَتْ عَنْ مُضَاعَفَةٍ

مِنَ الدُّرُوعِ وَعَنْ عَالٍ مِنَ الْأُطُمِ

79. *God's guardianship made extra armour*
needless, neither did they
need lofty castles.

Why now, Sohail, I'll tell you what I'll say.
There is no God but Allah, that I'll say.
Divine commission he must surely hold:
Were it not so, he never had prevailed
To raise Medina, and cast Mecca down.

AMHERST TYSSEN

95

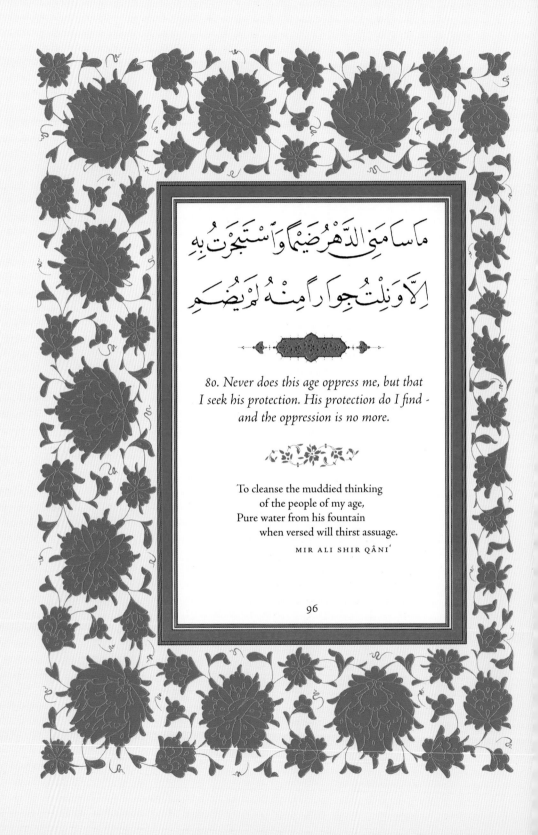

ماسا مِنَ الدَّهْرُ ضَيْماً وَاسْتَجَرْتُ بِه
اِلَّا وَنِلْتُ جِوارًا مِنْهُ لَمْ يَضِمِ

80. Never does this age oppress me, but that
I seek his protection. His protection do I find -
and the oppression is no more.

To cleanse the muddied thinking
of the people of my age,
Pure water from his fountain
when versed will thirst assuage.

MIR ALI SHIR QÂNI'

96

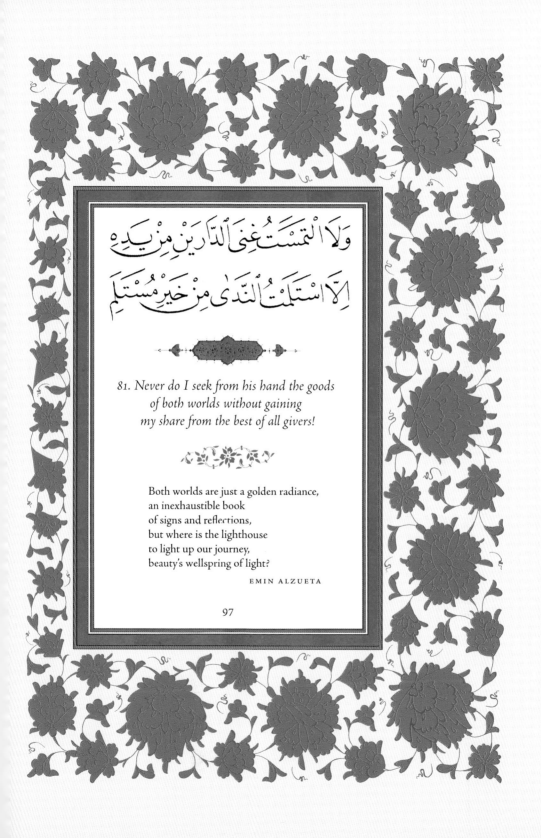

ولَا الْتَمَسْتُ غِنَى الدَّارَيْنِ مِنْ يَدِه

اِلَّا اسْتَلَمْتُ النَّدَى مِنْ خَيْرِ مُسْتَلَمِ

81. Never do I seek from his hand the goods
of both worlds without gaining
my share from the best of all givers!

Both worlds are just a golden radiance,
an inexhaustible book
of signs and reflections,
but where is the lighthouse
to light up our journey,
beauty's wellspring of light?

EMIN ALZUETA

97

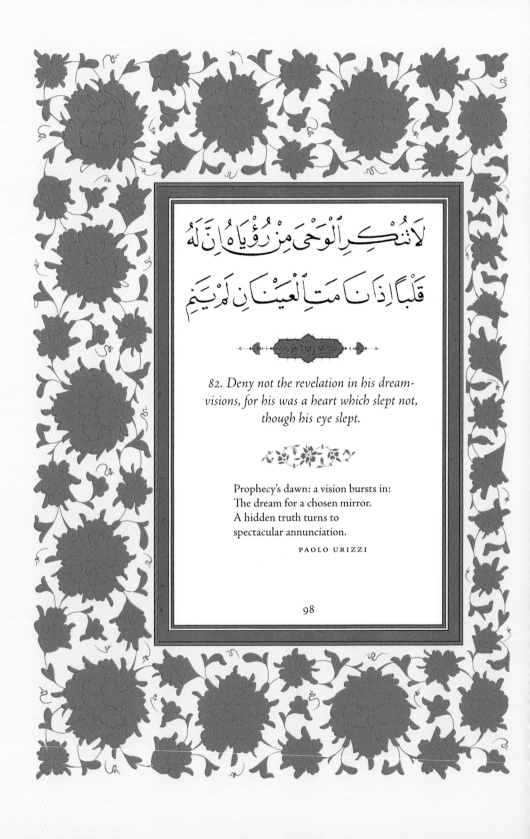

لَا تُنْكِرِ الْوَحْيَ مِنْ رُؤْيَاهُ اِنَّ لَهُ قَلْبًا اِذَا نَامَتِ الْعَيْنَانِ لَمْ يَنَمْ

82. Deny not the revelation in his dream-
visions, for his was a heart which slept not,
though his eye slept.

Prophecy's dawn: a vision bursts in:
The dream for a chosen mirror.
A hidden truth turns to
spectacular annunciation.

PAOLO URIZZI

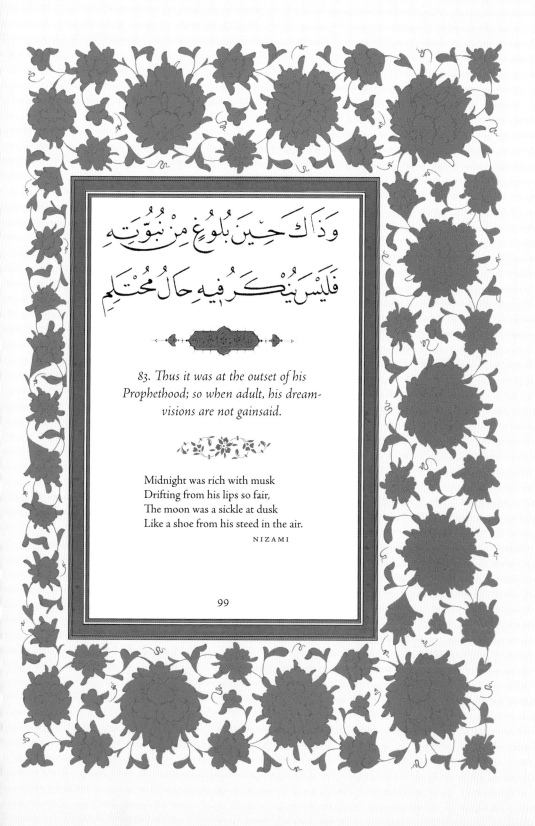

وَذَاكَ حِينَ بُلُوغٍ مِنْ نُبُوَّتِهِ

فَلَيْسَ يُنْكَرُ فِيهِ حَالُ مُحْتَلِمِ

83. *Thus it was at the outset of his Prophethood; so when adult, his dream-visions are not gainsaid.*

Midnight was rich with musk
Drifting from his lips so fair,
The moon was a sickle at dusk
Like a shoe from his steed in the air.

NIZAMI

99

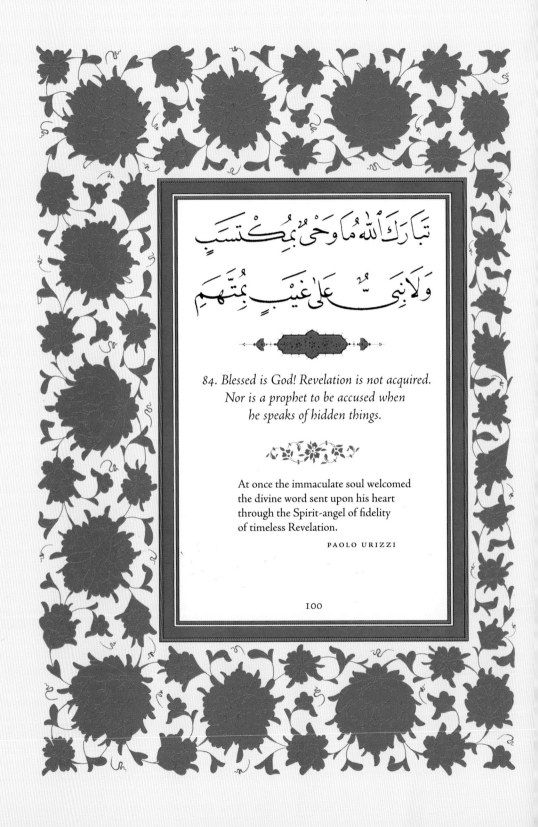

تَبَارَكَ اللهُ مَا وَحْيٌ بِمُكْتَسَبِ
وَلَا نَبِيٌّ عَلَى غَيْبٍ بِمُتَّهَمِ

84. Blessed is God! Revelation is not acquired.
Nor is a prophet to be accused when
he speaks of hidden things.

At once the immaculate soul welcomed
the divine word sent upon his heart
through the Spirit-angel of fidelity
of timeless Revelation.

PAOLO URIZZI

100

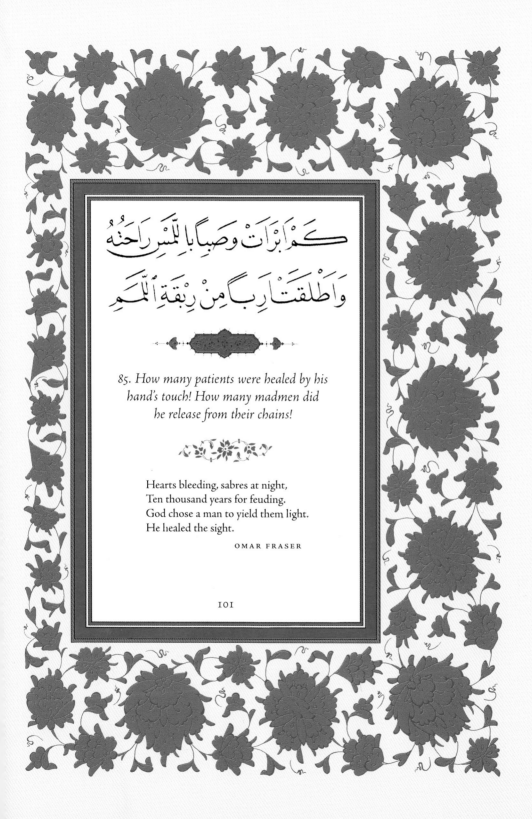

كَمْ بَرَأَتْ وَصِبًا بِاللَّمْسِ رَاحَتُهُ
وَأَطْلَقَتْ أَرَبًا مِنْ رِبْقَةِ اللَّمَمِ

85. How many patients were healed by his
hand's touch! How many madmen did
he release from their chains!

Hearts bleeding, sabres at night,
Ten thousand years for feuding.
God chose a man to yield them light.
He healed the sight.

OMAR FRASER

101

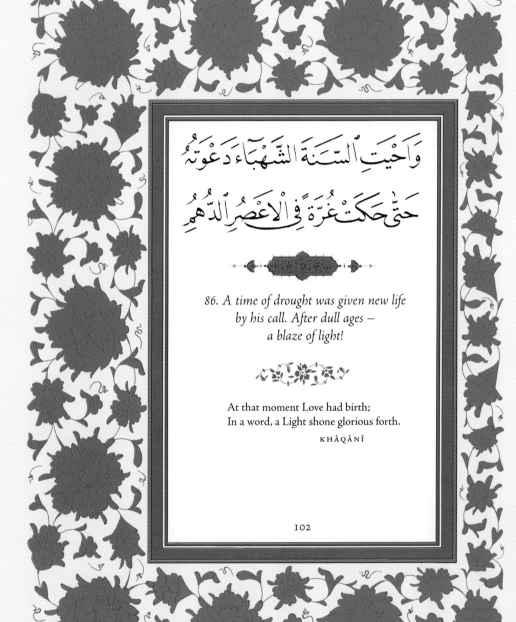

وَأَحْيَتِ ٱلسَّنَةَ ٱلشَّهْبَآءَ دَعْوَتُهُ

حَتَّىٰ حَكَتْ غُرَّةً فِي ٱلْاَعْصُرِ ٱلدُّهْمِ

86. *A time of drought was given new life*
by his call. After dull ages –
a blaze of light!

At that moment Love had birth;
In a word, a Light shone glorious forth.

KHÂQÂNÎ

102

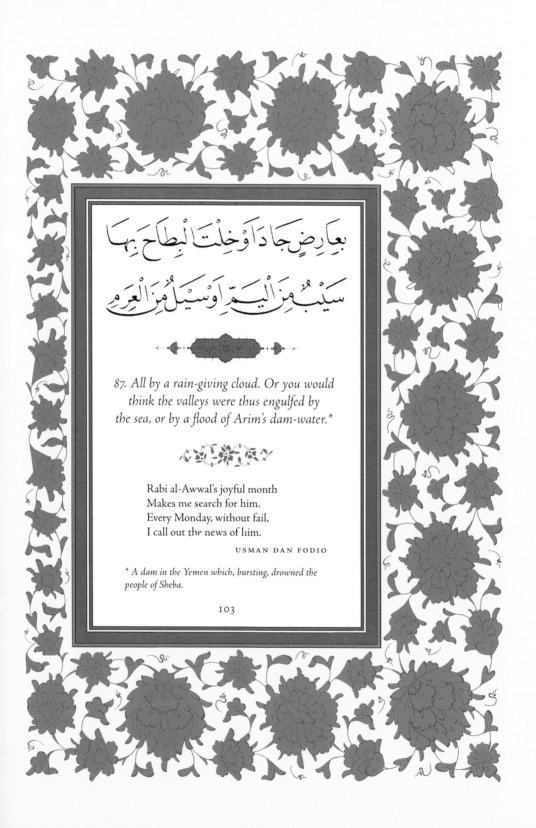

بِعَارِضٍ جَادَ اَوْخِلْتَ الْبِطَاحَ بِهَا

سَيْبٌ مِنَ الْيَمِّ اَوْسَيْلٌ مِنَ الْعَرِمِ

87. *All by a rain-giving cloud. Or you would*
think the valleys were thus engulfed by
*the sea, or by a flood of Arim's dam-water.**

Rabi al-Awwal's joyful month
Makes me search for him.
Every Monday, without fail,
I call out the news of him.

USMAN DAN FODIO

* *A dam in the Yemen which, bursting, drowned the*
people of Sheba.

103

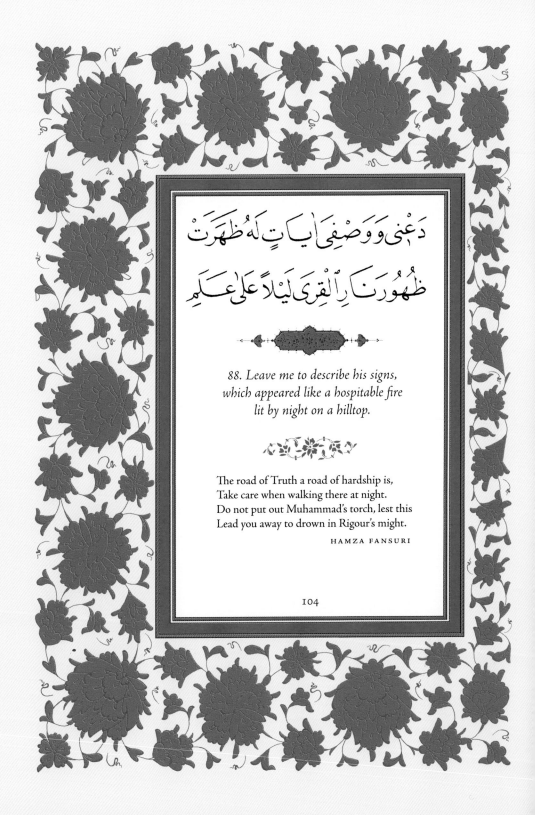

دَعْنِى وَوَصْفِى اٰيَاتٍ لَهُ ظَهَرَتْ

ظُهُورَنَارِ الْقِرَى لَيْلًا عَلَى عَلَمِ

88. Leave me to describe his signs,
which appeared like a hospitable fire
lit by night on a hilltop.

The road of Truth a road of hardship is,
Take care when walking there at night.
Do not put out Muhammad's torch, lest this
Lead you away to drown in Rigour's might.

HAMZA FANSURI

104

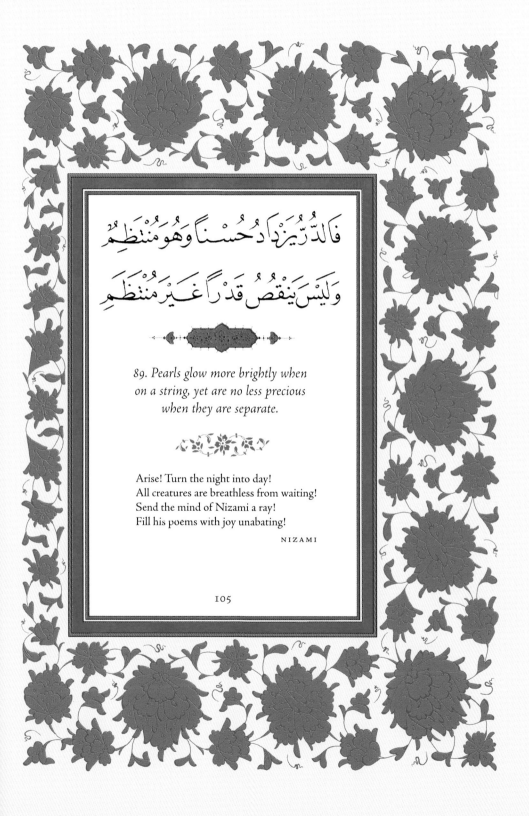

فَالدُّرُّ يَزْدَادُ حُسْنًا وَهُوَ مُنْتَظِمٌ

وَلَيْسَ يَنْقُصُ قَدْرًا غَيْرَ مُنْتَظِمِ

89. *Pearls glow more brightly when on a string, yet are no less precious when they are separate.*

Arise! Turn the night into day!
All creatures are breathless from waiting!
Send the mind of Nizami a ray!
Fill his poems with joy unabating!

NIZAMI

105

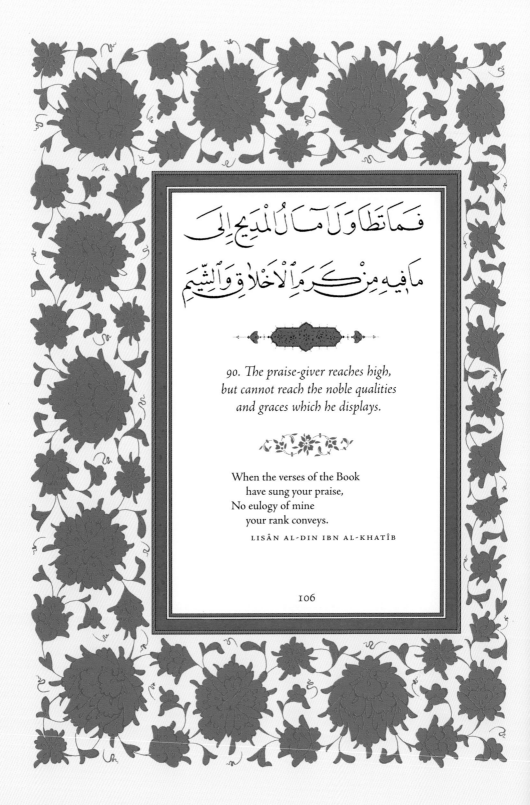

فَمَا تَطَاوَلَ آمَالُ الْمَدِيحِ إِلَى

مَا فِيهِ مِنْ كَرَمِ الْأَخْلَاقِ وَالشِّيَمِ

90. The praise-giver reaches high,
but cannot reach the noble qualities
and graces which he displays.

When the verses of the Book
have sung your praise,
No eulogy of mine
your rank conveys.

LISÂN AL-DIN IBN AL-KHATÎB

106

آيَاتُ حَقٍّ مِنَ الرَّحْمَنِ مُحْدَثَةٌ

قَدِيمَةٌ صِفَةُ الْمَوْصُوفِ بِالْقِدَمِ

91. *Though they are renewed, signs of truth*
from the Merciful precede time itself;
their quality is that of Him who is eternal.

Thy rising to God
proved thy lofty degree.
Descending to earth,
His own word greeted thee.

FUZULI

107

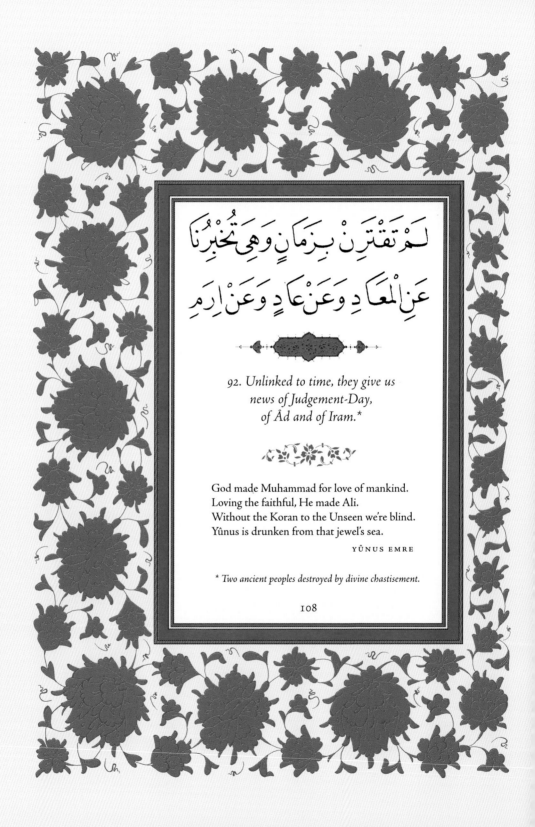

لَمْ تَقْتَرِنْ بِـزَمَانٍ وَهِيَ تُخْبِرُنَا

عَنِ الْمَعَادِ وَعَنْ عَادٍ وَعَنْ اِرَمِ

92. *Unlinked to time, they give us*
news of Judgement-Day,
*of Âd and of Iram.**

God made Muhammad for love of mankind.
Loving the faithful, He made Ali.
Without the Koran to the Unseen we're blind.
Yûnus is drunken from that jewel's sea.

YÛNUS EMRE

* *Two ancient peoples destroyed by divine chastisement.*

دَامَتْ لَدَيْنَا فَفَاقَتْ كُلَّ مُعْجِزَةٍ

مِنَ النَّبِيِّينَ اِذْ جَاءَتْ وَلَمْ تَدُمِ

93. *Constantly with us, above every*
miracle of prophets of old,
which came and went.

If we compare the Prophets to a rose
Then you are all the fragrance of that rose.
If they are like the shining sun of day,
Then you are as its glorious golden ray.

MAWLANA MUHAMMAD NANOTVI

109

مُحْكَمَاتٌ فَمَا تُبْقِينَ مِنْ شُبَهِ

لِذِى شِقَاقٍ وَمَا تَبْغِينَ مِنْ حَكَمِ

94. *Clear and strong, these signs leave*
no doubt to be stirred up by the mischievous,
and need no arbiter.

But masterfully, the angel showed him
and showed him, the letters on his page.
Again, tirelessly demanding: Read!

RILKE

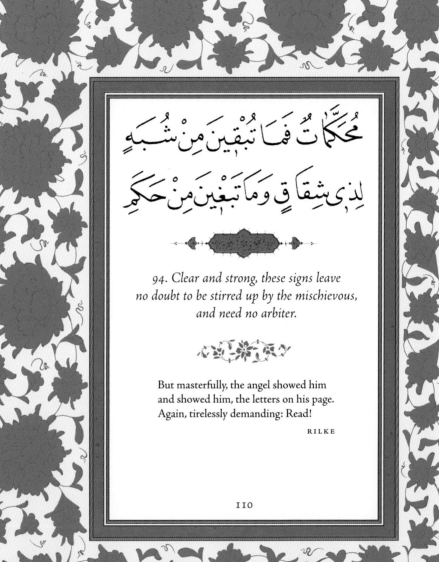

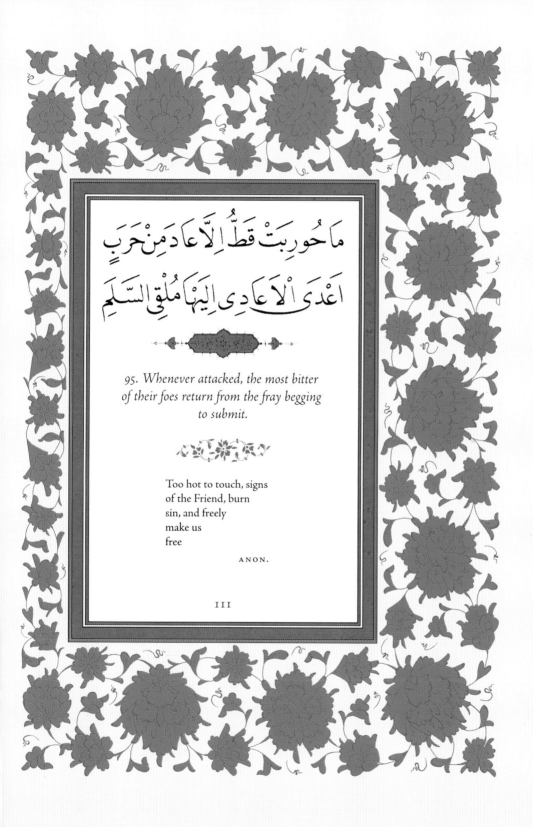

مَا حُورِبَتْ قَطُّ الَّا عَادَ مِنْ حَرَبٍ

اَعْدَى الْاَعَادِى اِلَيْهَا مُلْقِى السَّلَمْ

95. *Whenever attacked, the most bitter*
of their foes return from the fray begging
to submit.

Too hot to touch, signs
of the Friend, burn
sin, and freely
make us
free

ANON.

113

رَدَّتْ بِبَلاغَتِهَا دَعْوَى مُعَارِضِهَا

رَدَّ الْغَيُورِ يَدَ الْجَانِي عَنِ الْحُرَمِ

96. Their eloquence routs their enemy's claims,
as a zealous man protects his wife
from an assailant.

Whatever verse is read
Is a heart-beguiling bride.
If a groom that bride would wed -
Let him move her veil aside.

IBN 'ATA' ILLÂH

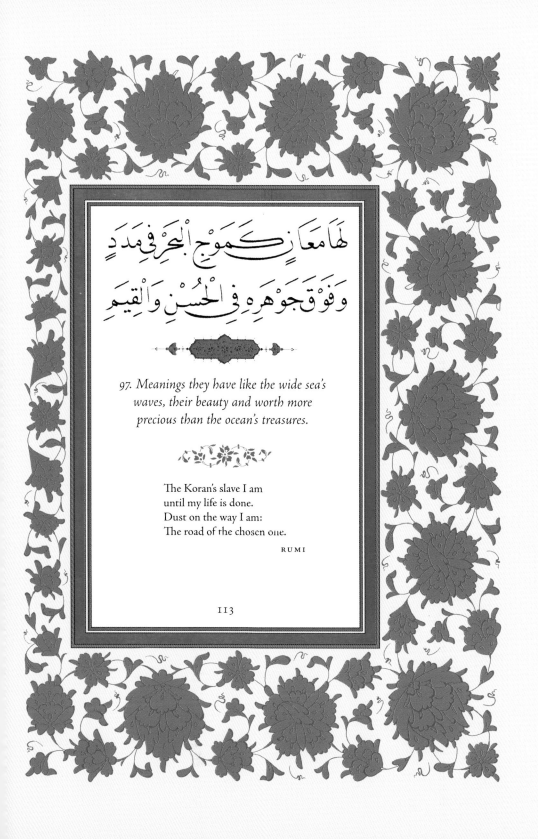

هَامَعَازِ كَمَوْجِ الْبَحْرِ فِى مَدَدِ

وَفَوْقَ جَوْهَرِهِ فِى الْحُسْنِ وَالْقِيَمِ

97. Meanings they have like the wide sea's
waves, their beauty and worth more
precious than the ocean's treasures.

The Koran's slave I am
until my life is done.
Dust on the way I am:
The road of the chosen one.

RUMI

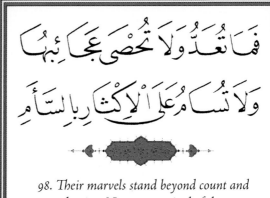

فَمَا تُعَدُّ وَلَا تُحْصَى عَجَائِبُهَا
وَلَا تُسَامُ عَلَى الْإِكْثَارِ بِالسَّأَمِ

98. *Their marvels stand beyond count and*
reckoning. None grows tired of them,
however oft-repeated.

We hail thee, Allah's prophet true,
Of prophecy the seal.
We read with reverence the book
Thou wast sent to reveal.

ABDULLAH QUILLIAM BEY

114

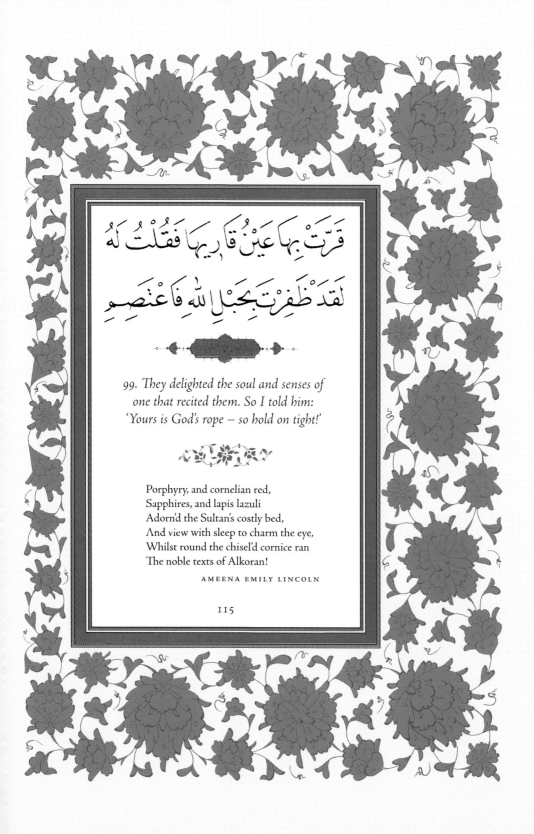

قَرَّتْ بِهَا عَيْنُ قَارِيهَا فَقُلْتُ لَهُ
لَقَدْ ظَفِرْتَ بِحَبْلِ اللهِ فَاعْتَصِمِ

99. *They delighted the soul and senses of*
one that recited them. So I told him:
'Yours is God's rope – so hold on tight!'

Porphyry, and cornelian red,
Sapphires, and lapis lazuli
Adorn'd the Sultan's costly bed,
And view with sleep to charm the eye,
Whilst round the chisel'd cornice ran
The noble texts of Alkoran!

AMEENA EMILY LINCOLN

115

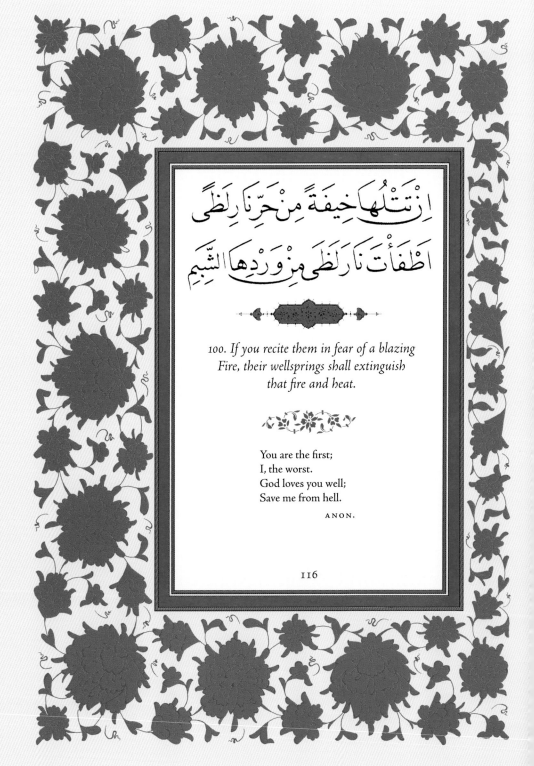

اِنْ تَتْلُهَا خِيفَةً مِنْ حَرِّ نَارِ لَظَى
اَطْفَأْتَ نَارَ لَظَى مِنْ وِرْدِهَا الشَّبِمِ

100. *If you recite them in fear of a blazing*
Fire, their wellsprings shall extinguish
that fire and heat.

You are the first;
I, the worst.
God loves you well;
Save me from hell.

ANON.

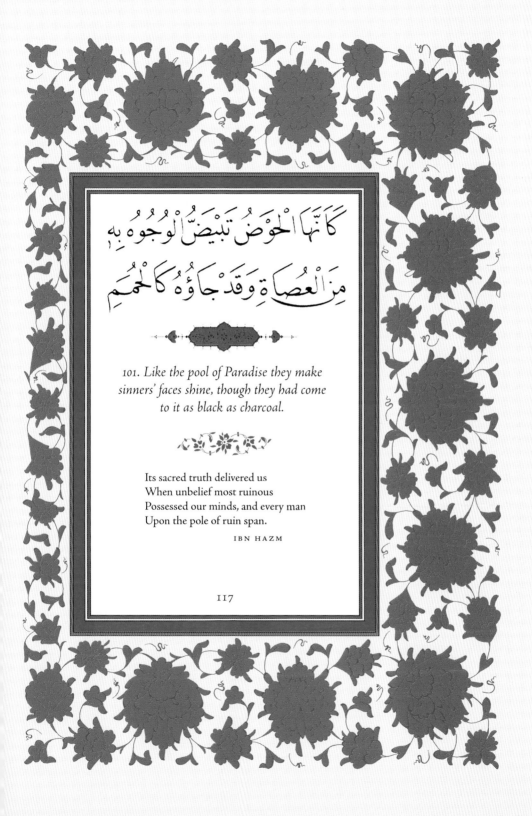

كَأَنَّهَا الْحَوْضُ تَبْيَضُّ الْوُجُوهُ بِهِ
مِنَ الْعُصَاةِ وَقَدْ جَاؤُهُ كَالْحُمَمِ

101. Like the pool of Paradise they make
sinners' faces shine, though they had come
to it as black as charcoal.

Its sacred truth delivered us
When unbelief most ruinous
Possessed our minds, and every man
Upon the pole of ruin span.

IBN HAZM

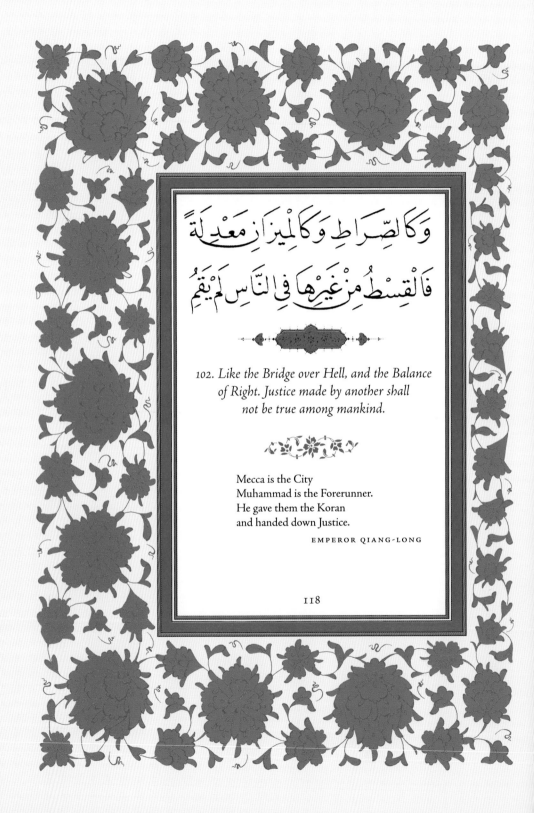

وَكَالصِّرَاطِ وَكَالْمِيزَانِ مَعْدِلَةً
فَالْقِسْطُ مِنْ غَيْرِهَا فِى النَّاسِ لَمْ يَقُمِ

102. *Like the Bridge over Hell, and the Balance*
of Right. Justice made by another shall
not be true among mankind.

Mecca is the City
Muhammad is the Forerunner.
He gave them the Koran
and handed down Justice.

EMPEROR QIANG-LONG

118

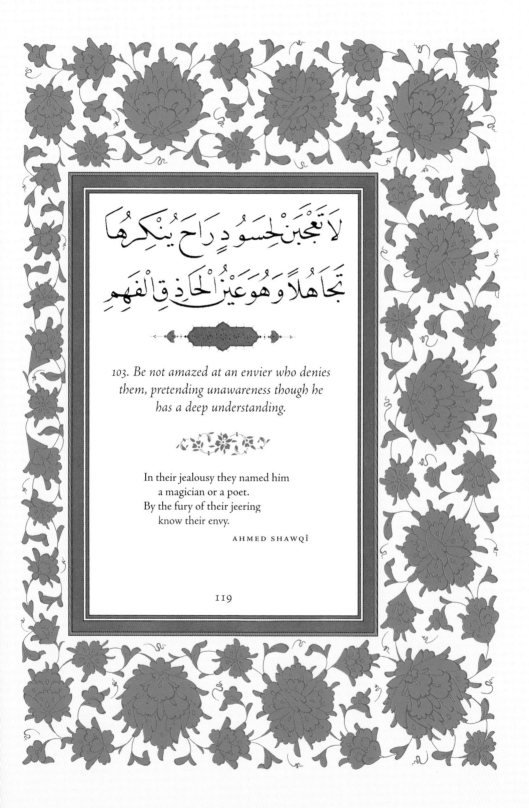

لَا تَعْجَبَنْ لِحَسُودٍ رَاحَ يُنْكِرُهَا

تَجَاهُلًا وَهُوَ عَيْنُ الْحَاذِقِ الْفَهِمِ

103. Be not amazed at an envier who denies
them, pretending unawareness though he
has a deep understanding.

In their jealousy they named him
a magician or a poet.
By the fury of their jeering
know their envy.

AHMED SHAWQÎ

119

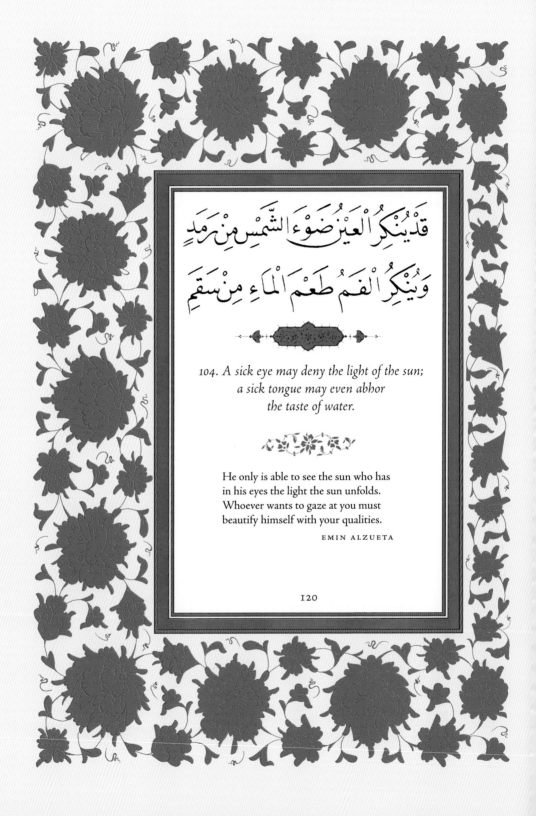

قَدْ يُنْكِرُ الْعَيْنُ ضَوْءَ الشَّمْسِ مِنْ رَمَدٍ

وَيُنْكِرُ الْفَمُ طَعْمَ الْمَاءِ مِنْ سَقَمٍ

104. *A sick eye may deny the light of the sun;*
a sick tongue may even abhor
the taste of water.

He only is able to see the sun who has
in his eyes the light the sun unfolds.
Whoever wants to gaze at you must
beautify himself with your qualities.

EMIN ALZUETA

120

يَا خَيْرَ مَنْ يَمَّمَ الْعَافُونَ سَاحَتَهُ

سَعْيًا وَفَوْقَ مَتُونِ الْأَيْنُقِ الرُّسُمِ

105. *O best of those whose courtyard is sought*
by the needy; they run, or ride the
backs of tireless camels.

A vision of thy beauty, beloved of the world,
Would turn our sordid clay to purest gold.
Such a lamp art thou, that on Ascension's eve,
Each broken mortal spirit was consoled

AHMET PAŞA

121

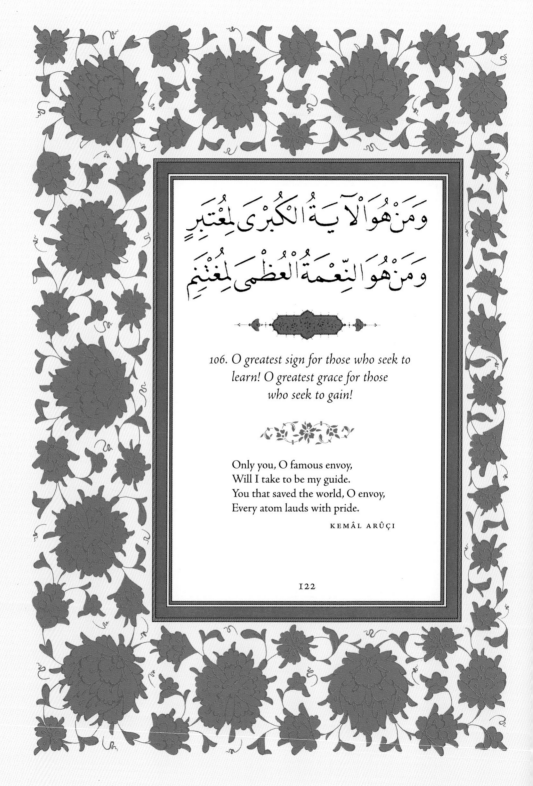

وَمِنْهُوَ الْآيَةُ الْكُبْرَى لِمُعْتَبِرٍ
وَمِنْهُوَ النِّعْمَةُ الْعُظْمَى لِمُغْتَنِمٍ

106. *O greatest sign for those who seek to*
learn! O greatest grace for those
who seek to gain!

Only you, O famous envoy,
Will I take to be my guide.
You that saved the world, O envoy,
Every atom lauds with pride.

KEMÂL ARÛÇI

122

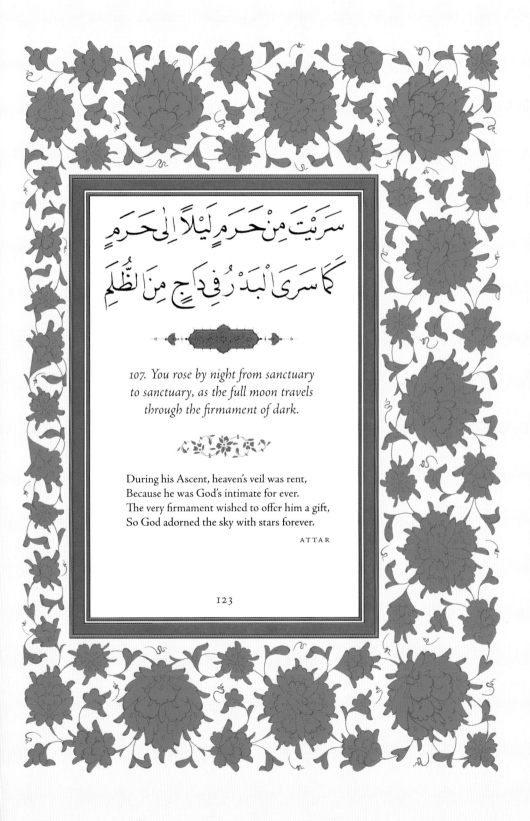

سَرَيْتَ مِنْ حَرَمٍ لَيْلاً إِلَى حَرَمٍ

كَمَا سَرَى الْبَدْرُ فِي دَاجٍ مِنَ الظُّلَمِ

*107. You rose by night from sanctuary
to sanctuary, as the full moon travels
through the firmament of dark.*

During his Ascent, heaven's veil was rent,
Because he was God's intimate for ever.
The very firmament wished to offer him a gift,
So God adorned the sky with stars forever.

ATTAR

123

وَبِتَّ تَرْقَى إِلَى اَنْ نِلْتَ مَنْزِلَةً
مِنْ قَابَ قَوْسَيْنِ لَمْ تُدْرَكُ وَلَمْ تُرَمِ

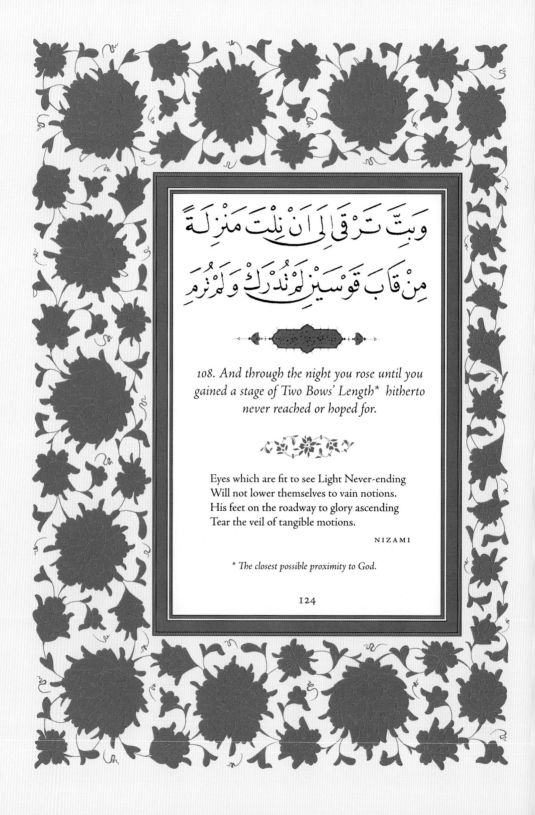

108. *And through the night you rose until you*
gained a stage of Two Bows' Length* hitherto
never reached or hoped for.

Eyes which are fit to see Light Never-ending
Will not lower themselves to vain notions.
His feet on the roadway to glory ascending
Tear the veil of tangible motions.

NIZAMI

* *The closest possible proximity to God.*

124

وَقَدَّمَتْكَ جَمِيعُ الْاَنْبِيَاءِ بِهَا
وَالرُّسْلِ تَقْدِيمَ مَخْدُومٍ عَلَى خَدَمٍ

109. There all of the Prophets gave you
    precedence. The Messengers too, as
    servants give way to their master.

When you, like Moses, came into
    the pulpit of the sky,
The fourth high sphere heard Jesus speak:
    'Welcome!' came the cry.

URFI

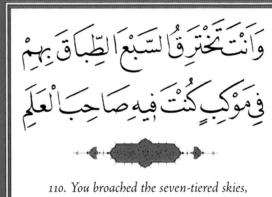

وَاَنْتَ تَخْتَرِقُ السَّبْعَ الطِّبَاقَ بِهِمْ

فِي مَوْكِبٍ كُنْتَ فِيهِ صَاحِبَ الْعَلَمْ

110. You broached the seven-tiered skies,
with them behind you, in a procession
where you were the standard-bearer!

On the steed of love, God's prophet rose,
through the blazing heavens,
The messengers of old rose to salute him,
noble-browed, he blessed them all.

RUMI

126

حَتّىٓ إِذَا الْمُرْتَدِعَ شَأُوَّا الْمُسْتَبِقِ
مِنَ الدُّنُوِّ وَلَا مَرْقّى لِمُسْتَنِمِ

111. *Until your closeness left no space for*
others on the quest; nor summit for
others to attain.

When his religion gave light to the world,
The other rites halted and stayed, as God knows;
For what may become of the myriad stars
When over the world a new sunrise glows?

ATTAR

127

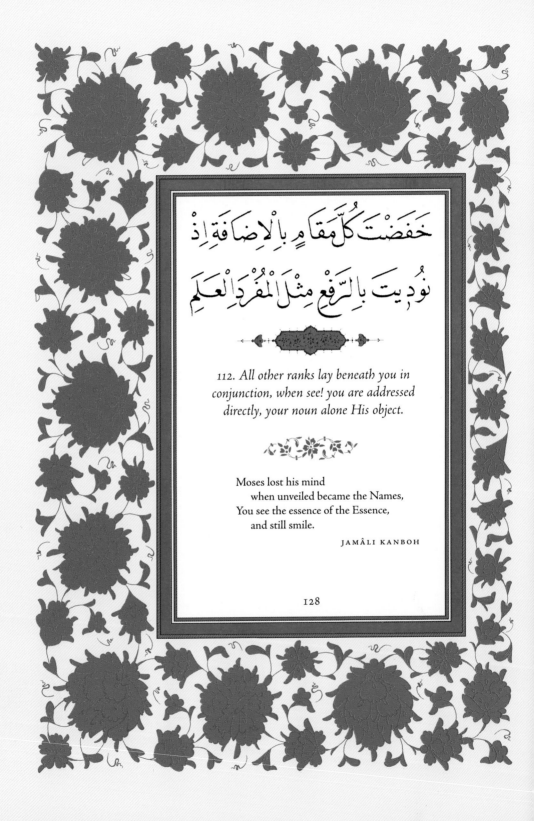

خَفَضْتَ كُلَّ مَقَامٍ بِالْإِضَافَةِ إِذْ
نُودِيتَ بِالرَّفْعِ مِثْلَ الْمُفْرَدِ الْعَلَمِ

112. *All other ranks lay beneath you in*
conjunction, when see! you are addressed
directly, your noun alone His object.

Moses lost his mind
when unveiled became the Names,
You see the essence of the Essence,
and still smile.

JAMÂLI KANBOH

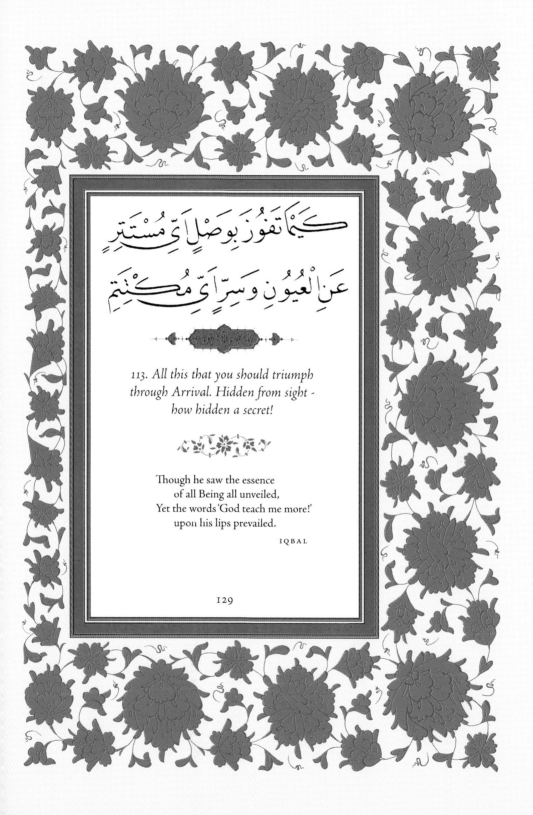

عَنِ الْعُيُونِ وَسِرَّاً مُكَنْتُمْ

كَيْمَا تَفُوزُ بِوَصْلٍ أَيْ مُسْتَتِرٍ

113. *All this that you should triumph*
through Arrival. Hidden from sight -
how hidden a secret!

Though he saw the essence
of all Being all unveiled,
Yet the words 'God teach me more!'
upon his lips prevailed.

IQBAL

129

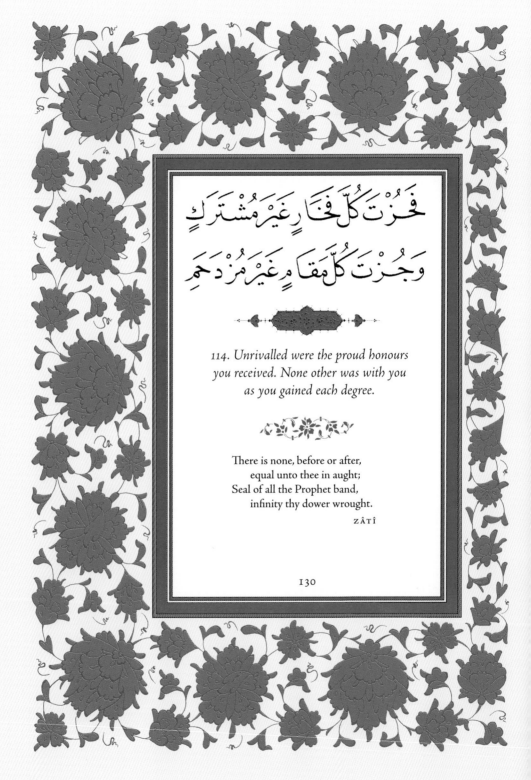

فَخُزْتَ كُلَّ فَخَارٍ غَيْرَ مُشْتَرَكٍ

وَجُزْتَ كُلَّ مَقَامٍ غَيْرَ مُزْدَحَمٍ

114. Unrivalled were the proud honours
you received. None other was with you
as you gained each degree.

There is none, before or after,
equal unto thee in aught;
Seal of all the Prophet band,
infinity thy dower wrought.

ZÂTÎ

130

وَجَلَّ مِقْدَارُ مَا وُلِّيتَ مِنْ رُتَبٍ

وَعَزَّ أَدْرَاكُ مَا أُوْلِيتَ مِنْ نِعَمِ

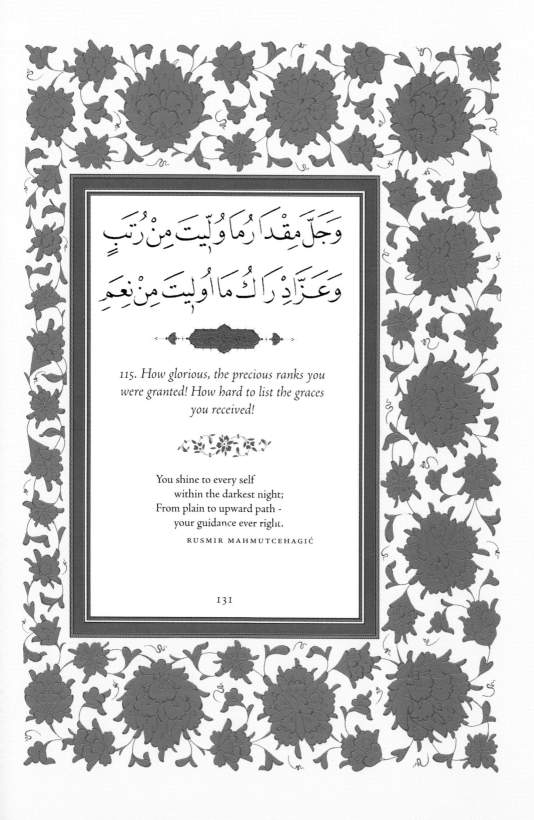

115. How glorious, the precious ranks you
were granted! How hard to list the graces
you received!

You shine to every self
within the darkest night;
From plain to upward path -
your guidance ever right.

RUSMIR MAHMUTCEHAGIĆ

131

بُشْرَى لَنَا مَعْشَرَ الْإِسْلَامِ إِنَّ لَنَا

مِنَ الْعِنَايَةِ رُكْنًا غَيْرَ مُنْهَدِمِ

116. *Good news for us, people of Islam!*
For we possess a pillar of God's care
that shall not be overthrown.

All Prophecy lacked the estate of one brick,
A gap of greatest sanctity!
Our Prophet said: 'That precious gap,
I close for all eternity.'

ATTAR

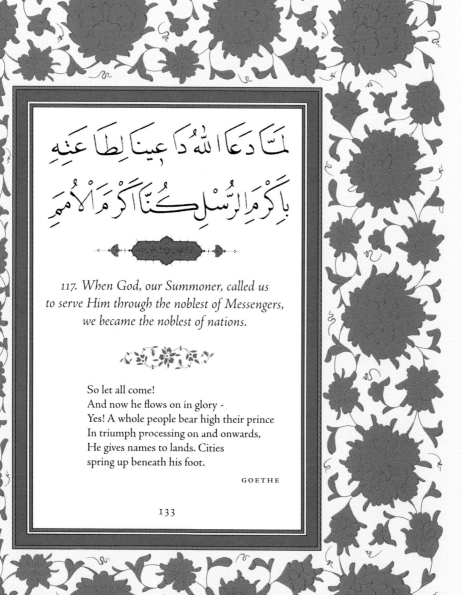

لَمَّا دَعَا اللهُ دَاعِينَا لِطَاعَتِهِ
بِأَكْرَمِ الرُّسْلِ كُنَّا أَكْرَمَ الْأُمَمِ

117. When God, our Summoner, called us
to serve Him through the noblest of Messengers,
we became the noblest of nations.

So let all come!
And now he flows on in glory –
Yes! A whole people bear high their prince
In triumph processing on and onwards,
He gives names to lands. Cities
spring up beneath his foot.

GOETHE

133

راعَتْ قُلُوبَ الْعِدَا اَنْبَاءُ بَعْثَتِهِ

كَنَبْاَةٍ اَجْفَلَتْ غُفْلًا مِنَ الْغَنَمِ

118. *News that he was sent made foemen*
quake, just as a lion's roar
shakes heedless sheep.

The word you bring from Him
the voice of the voiceless will be.
The balm you bring from Him
the cure for the wounded will be.

NIZAMI

135

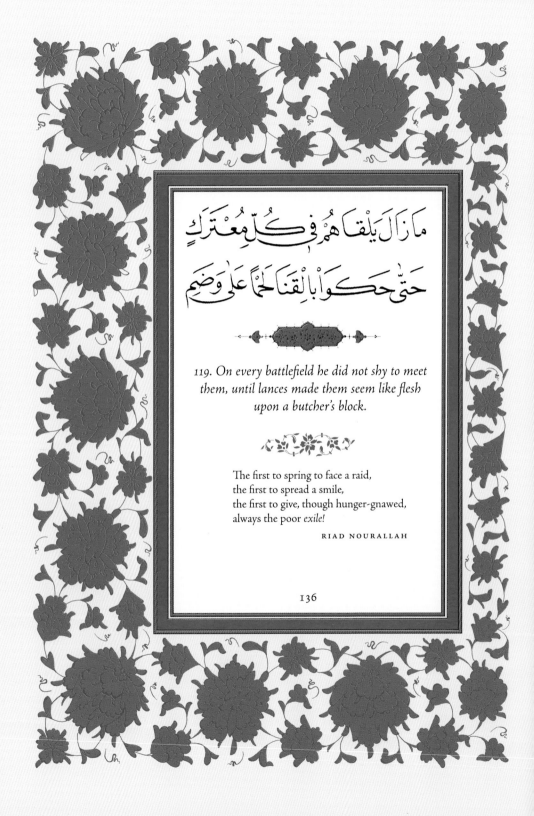

مَازَالَ يَلْقَاهُمْ فِى كُلِّ مُعْتَرَكِ

حَتّى حَكُوا بِالْقَنَا لَحْمًا عَلى وَضَمِ

119. *On every battlefield he did not shy to meet*
them, until lances made them seem like flesh
upon a butcher's block.

The first to spring to face a raid,
the first to spread a smile,
the first to give, though hunger-gnawed,
always the poor *exile!*

RIAD NOURALLAH

136

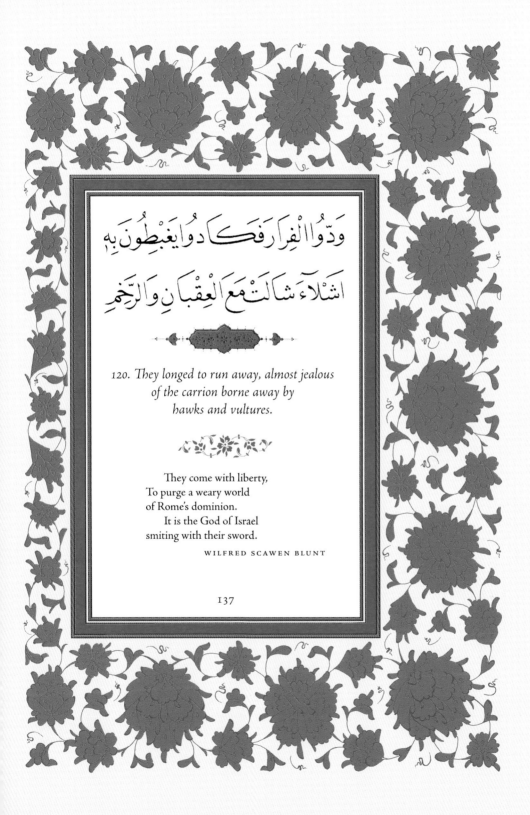

وَدُّوا الْفِرَارَ فَكَادُوا يَغْبِطُونَ بِهِ
اَشْلَاءَ شَالَتْ مَعَ الْعِقْبَانِ وَالرَّخَمِ

120. They longed to run away, almost jealous
of the carrion borne away by
hawks and vultures.

They come with liberty,
To purge a weary world
of Rome's dominion.
It is the God of Israel
smiting with their sword.

WILFRED SCAWEN BLUNT

137

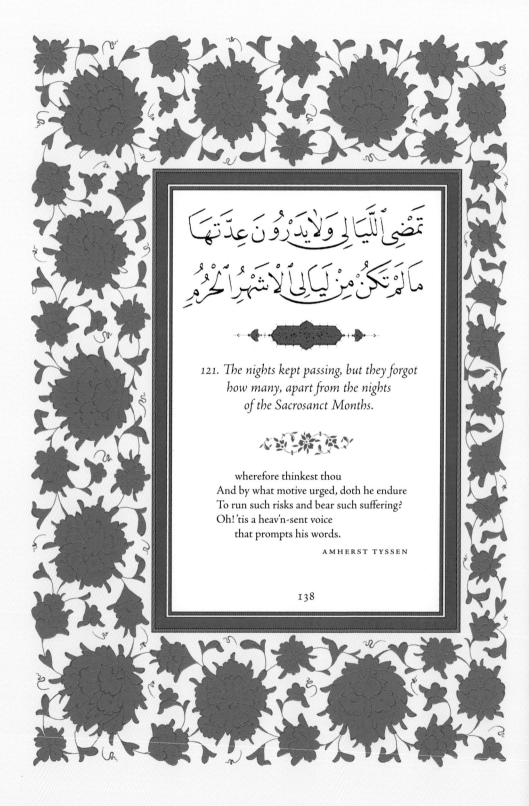

تَمْضِى ٱللَّيَالِى وَلَا يَدْرُونَ عِدَّتَهَا

مَا لَمْ تَكُنْ مِنْ لَيَالِى ٱلْأَشْهُرِ ٱلْحُرُمِ

121. *The nights kept passing, but they forgot*
how many, apart from the nights
of the Sacrosanct Months.

wherefore thinkest thou
And by what motive urged, doth he endure
To run such risks and bear such suffering?
Oh! 'tis a heav'n-sent voice
    that prompts his words.

AMHERST TYSSEN

138

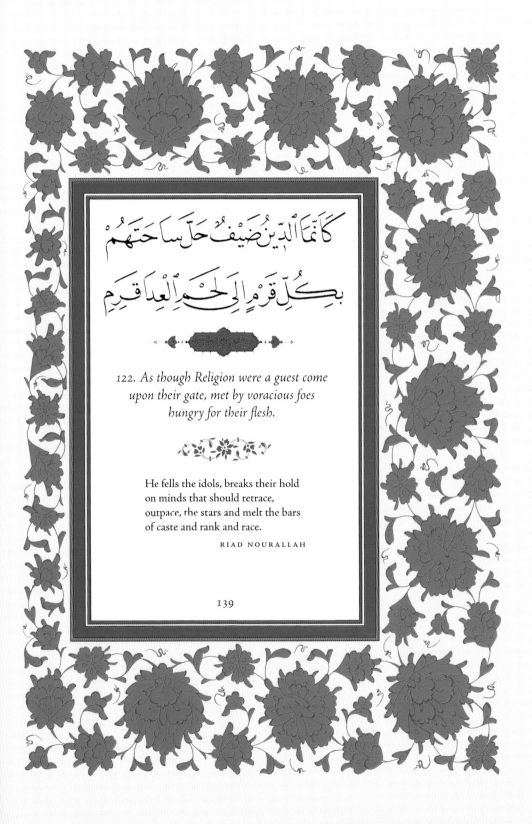

كَأَنَّمَا الدِّينُ ضَيْفٌ حَلَّ سَاحَتَهُمْ

بِكُلِّ قَرْمٍ إِلَى لَحْمِ الْعِدَا قَرِمِ

122. As though Religion were a guest come
upon their gate, met by voracious foes
hungry for their flesh.

He fells the idols, breaks their hold
on minds that should retrace,
outpace, the stars and melt the bars
of caste and rank and race.

RIAD NOURALLAH

139

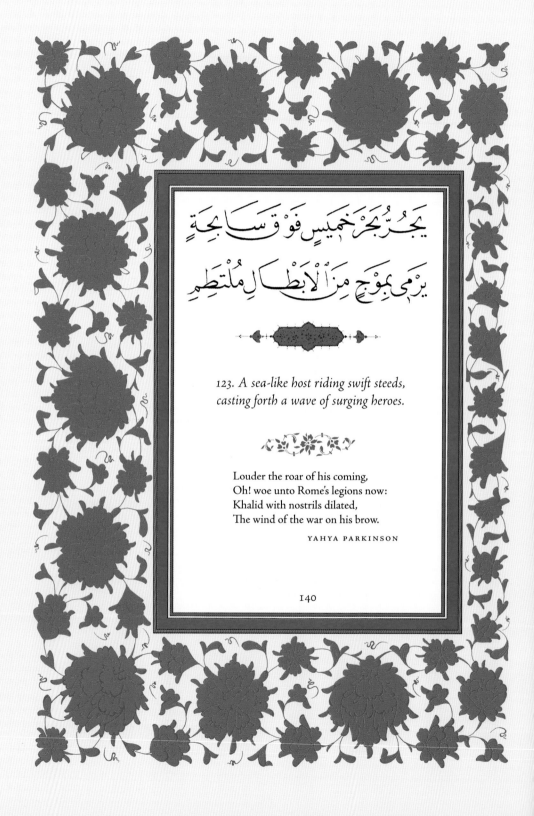

يَجُرُّ بَحْرَ خَمِيسٍ فَوْقَ سَابِحَةٍ

يَرْمِي بِمَوْجٍ مِنَ الْأَبْطَالِ مُلْتَطِمِ

123. A sea-like host riding swift steeds,
casting forth a wave of surging heroes.

Louder the roar of his coming,
Oh! woe unto Rome's legions now:
Khalid with nostrils dilated,
The wind of the war on his brow.

YAHYA PARKINSON

140

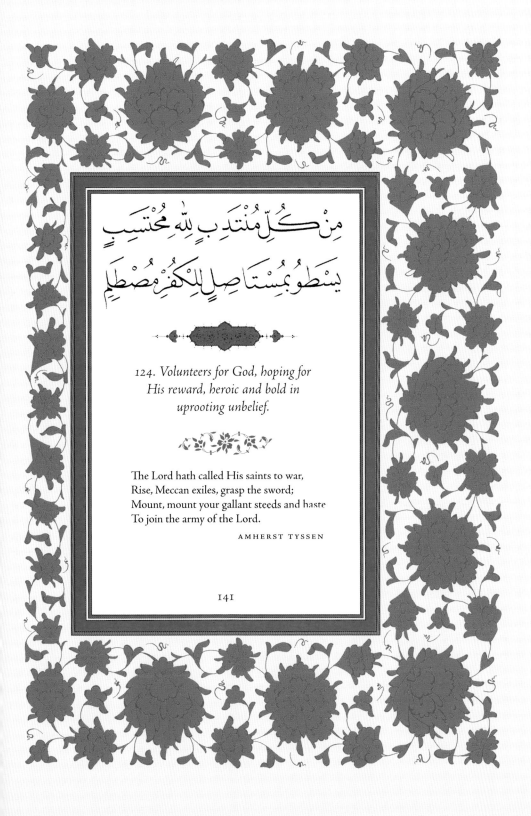

مِنْ كُلِّ مُنْتَدِبٍ لِلَّهِ مُحْتَسِبٍ

يَسْطُو بِمُسْتَأْصِلٍ لِلْكُفْرِ مُصْطَلِمِ

*124. Volunteers for God, hoping for
His reward, heroic and bold in
uprooting unbelief.*

The Lord hath called His saints to war,
Rise, Meccan exiles, grasp the sword;
Mount, mount your gallant steeds and haste
To join the army of the Lord.

AMHERST TYSSEN

141

حَتّى غَدَتْ مِلّةُ الْإِسْلَامِ وَهْيَ بِهِمْ

مِنْ بَعْدِ غُرْبَتِهَا مَوْصُولَةَ الرّحِمِ

125. Until the religion of Islam became,
through them, as one flesh, having once
been exiled and apart.

By the legacy of Amina's pure son
  Eastern man to Westerner drew nigh.
Once all at odds, he made our kinship one;
  Islam's sons we! No lineage more high.

AL-KUMAYT

142

مَكْفُولَةً أَبَدًا مِنْهُمْ بِخَيْرِ أَبِ

وَخَيْرِ بَعْلٍ فَلَمْ تَيْتَمْ وَلَمْ تَئِمِ

126. *Shielded for all time from evildoers*
by the best of fathers and husbands, so that
no longer were they orphans or widows.

Wherever there arises
a tumult of the worlds,
A Mercy for the Worlds
will surely come.

GHÂLIB

143

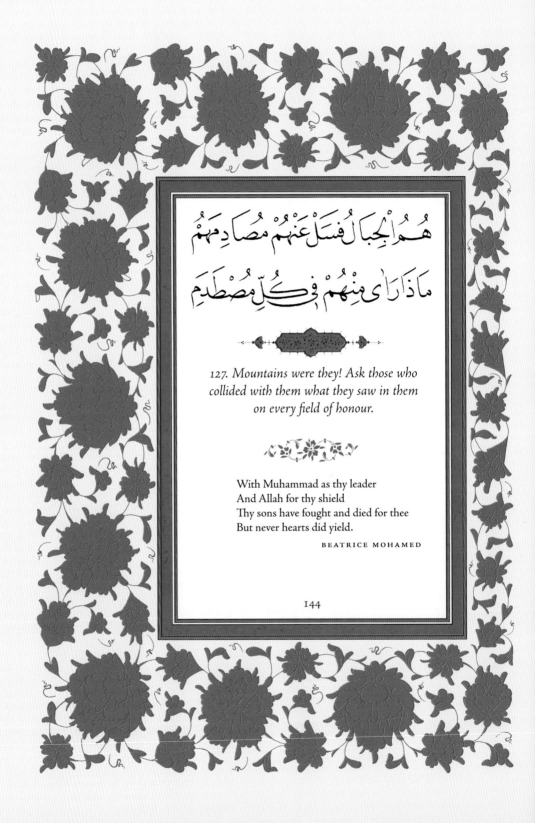

هُمُ الجِبَالُ فَسَلْ عَنْهُمْ مُصَادِمَهُمْ

مَاذَا رَأَى مِنْهُمْ فِى كُلِّ مُصْطَدَمِ

*127. Mountains were they! Ask those who
collided with them what they saw in them
on every field of honour.*

With Muhammad as thy leader
And Allah for thy shield
Thy sons have fought and died for thee
But never hearts did yield.

BEATRICE MOHAMED

144

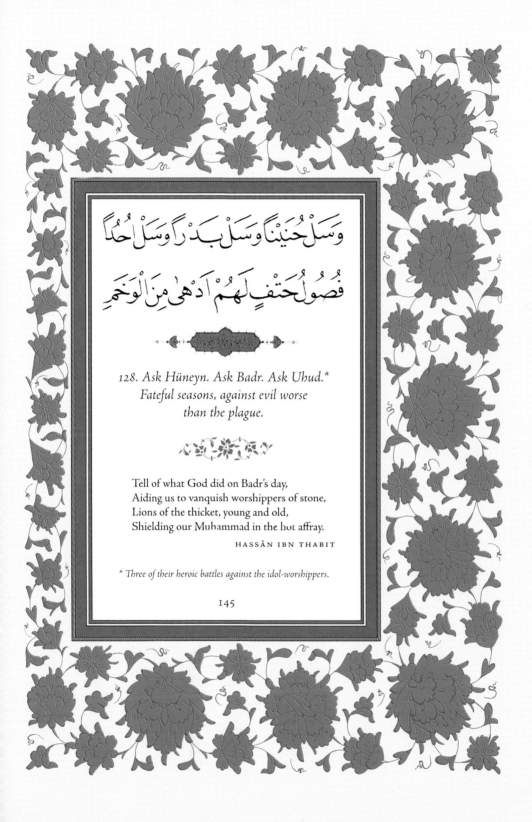

وَسَلْ حُنَيْنًا وَسَلْ بَدْرًا وَسَلْ أُحُدَا
فُصُولُ حَتْفٍ لَهُمْ أَدْهَى مِنَ الْوَخَمِ

128. *Ask Hüneyn. Ask Badr. Ask Uhud.*[*]
Fateful seasons, against evil worse
than the plague.

Tell of what God did on Badr's day,
Aiding us to vanquish worshippers of stone,
Lions of the thicket, young and old,
Shielding our Muhammad in the hot affray.

HASSÂN IBN THABIT

[*] *Three of their heroic battles against the idol-worshippers.*

145

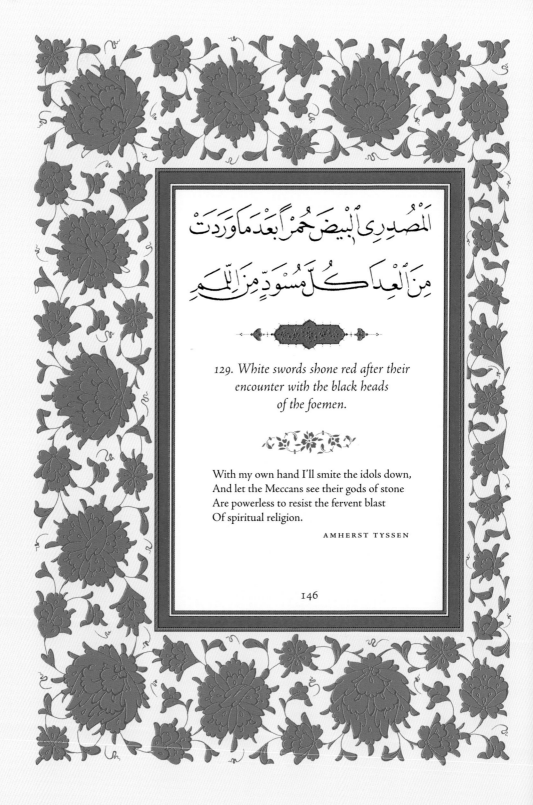

المُصْدِرِى الْبِيضَ حُمْرًا بَعْدَ مَا وَرَدَتْ

مِنَ الْعِدَا كُلَّ مُسْوَدٍّ مِنَ اللَّمَمِ

129. *White swords shone red after their*
encounter with the black heads
of the foemen.

With my own hand I'll smite the idols down,
And let the Meccans see their gods of stone
Are powerless to resist the fervent blast
Of spiritual religion.

AMHERST TYSSEN

146

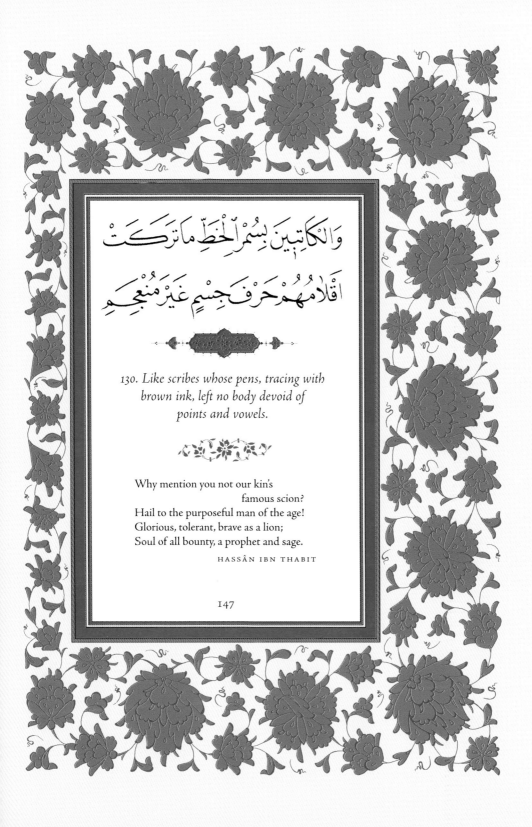

والكاتِبِينَ بِسُمرِ الخَطِّ ماتركَتْ
اقلامُهُمْ حرفَ جِسْمٍ غيرَ مُنعَجِمِ

130. *Like scribes whose pens, tracing with*
brown ink, left no body devoid of
points and vowels.

Why mention you not our kin's
          famous scion?
Hail to the purposeful man of the age!
Glorious, tolerant, brave as a lion;
Soul of all bounty, a prophet and sage.

HASSÂN IBN THABIT

147

شَاكِي ٱلسِّلَاحِ لَهُمْ سِيمَى تُمَيِّزُهُمْ

وَٱلْوَرْدُ يَمْتَازُ بِٱلسِّيمَى عَنِ ٱلسَّلَمِ

131. *In shining armour, theirs was a sign*
which set them apart, just as a rosebush may
be distinguished from an acacia.

Where'er the tale of Mecca won
    By Moslem arms is told in story,
There shall the Moslem strain be sung –
    To Thee, O Lord, we give the glory.

AMHERST TYSSEN

148

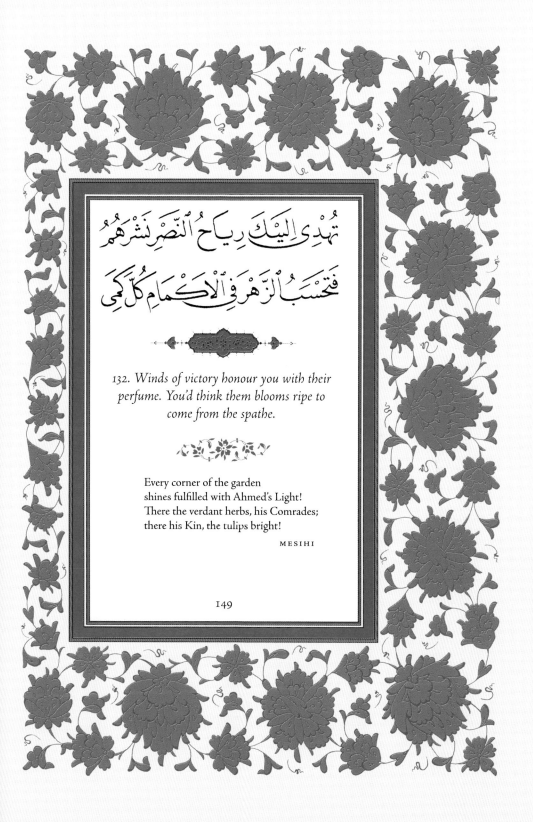

تُهْدِى اِلَيْكَ رِياحُ النَّصْرِ نَشْرَهُمُ

فَتَحْسَبُ الزَّهْرَ فِى الْاَكْمَامِ كُلَّ كمى

132. *Winds of victory honour you with their*
perfume. You'd think them blooms ripe to
come from the spathe.

Every corner of the garden
shines fulfilled with Ahmed's Light!
There the verdant herbs, his Comrades;
there his Kin, the tulips bright!

MESIHI

149

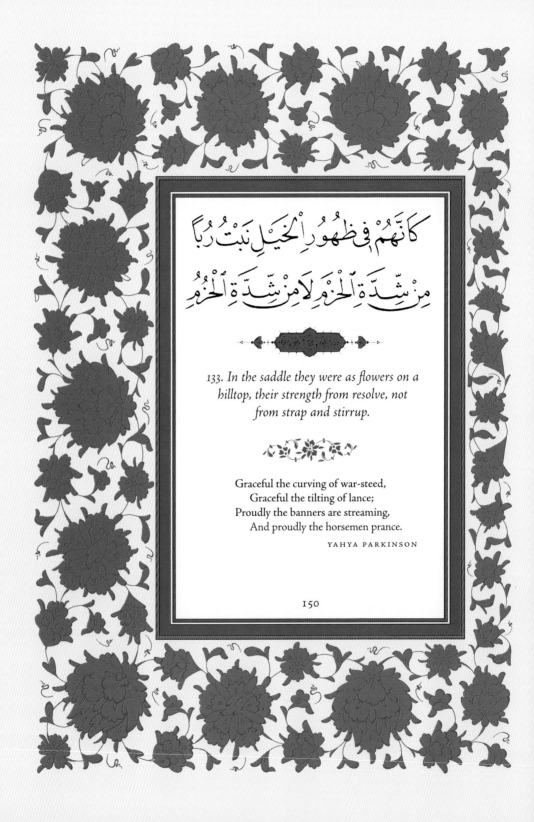

كَأَنَّهُمْ فِى ظُهُورِ الْخَيْلِ نَبْتٌ رُبَا
مِنْ شِدَّةِ الْحَزْمِ لَا مِنْ شِدَّةِ الْحُزُمِ

133. *In the saddle they were as flowers on a*
hilltop, their strength from resolve, not
from strap and stirrup.

Graceful the curving of war-steed,
Graceful the tilting of lance;
Proudly the banners are streaming,
And proudly the horsemen prance.

YAHYA PARKINSON

150

طَارَتْ قُلُوبُ الْعِدَا مِنْ بَأْسِهِمْ فَرَقًا

فَمَا تُفَرِّقُ بَيْنَ الْبُهْمِ وَالْبُهْمِ

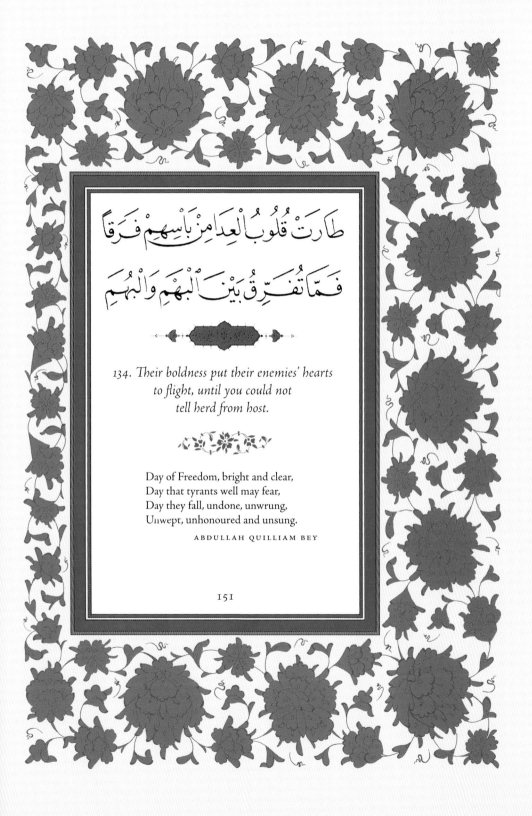

134. *Their boldness put their enemies' hearts*
to flight, until you could not
tell herd from host.

Day of Freedom, bright and clear,
Day that tyrants well may fear,
Day they fall, undone, unwrung,
Unwept, unhonoured and unsung.

ABDULLAH QUILLIAM BEY

151

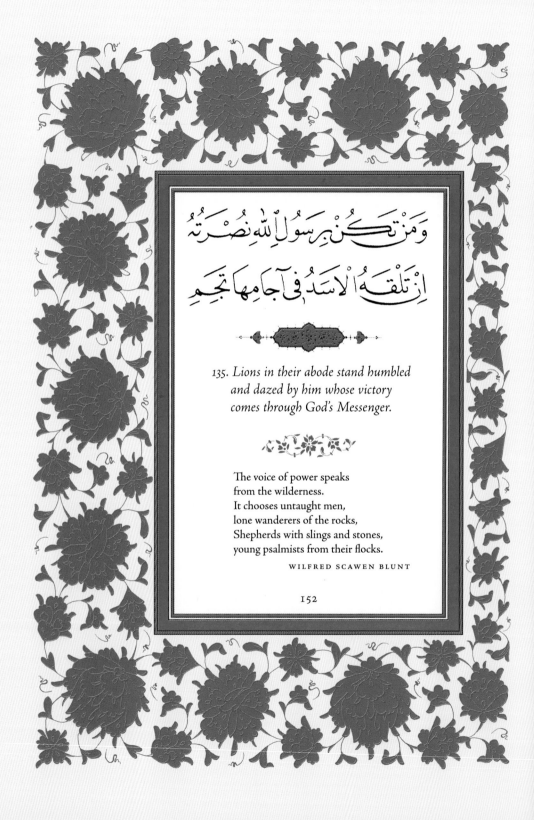

وَمَنْ تَكُنْ بِرَسُولِ اللَّهِ نُصْرَتُهُ
اِنْ تَلْقَهُ الْأُسُدُ فِى آجَامِهَا تَجِمِ

135. *Lions in their abode stand humbled*
and dazed by him whose victory
comes through God's Messenger.

The voice of power speaks
from the wilderness.
It chooses untaught men,
lone wanderers of the rocks,
Shepherds with slings and stones,
young psalmists from their flocks.

WILFRED SCAWEN BLUNT

152

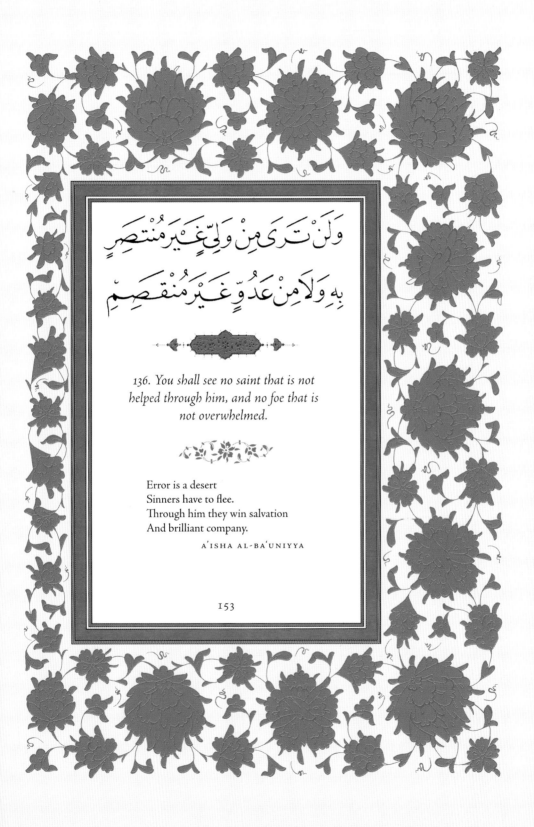

وَلَنْ تَرَى مِنْ وَلِيٍّ غَيْرَ مُنْتَصِرٍ

بِهِ وَلَا مِنْ عَدُوٍّ غَيْرَ مُنْقَصِمِ

136. *You shall see no saint that is not helped through him, and no foe that is not overwhelmed.*

Error is a desert
Sinners have to flee.
Through him they win salvation
And brilliant company.

A'ISHA AL-BA'UNIYYA

153

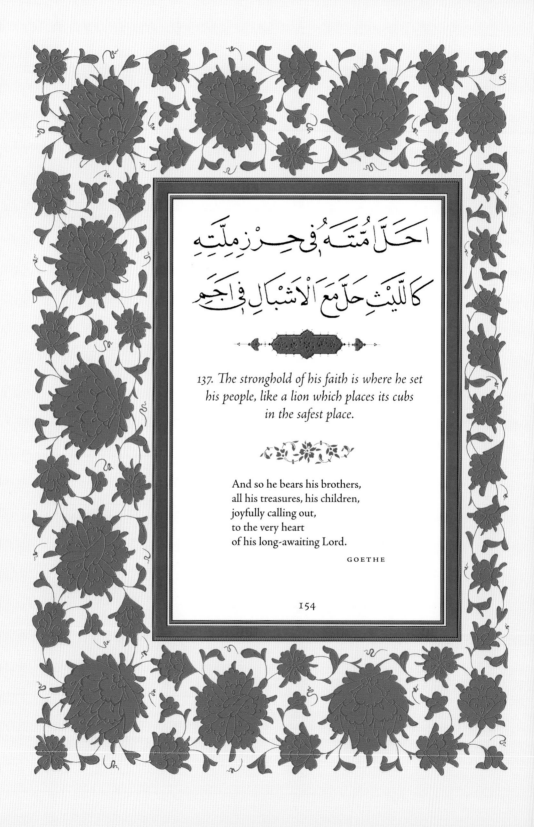

احَلَّ اُمَّتَه فى حِرْزِ مِلَّتِه

كَاللَّيْثِ حَلَّ مَعَ الْاَشْبَالِ فى اجَمِ

137. *The stronghold of his faith is where he set*
his people, like a lion which places its cubs
in the safest place.

And so he bears his brothers,
all his treasures, his children,
joyfully calling out,
to the very heart
of his long-awaiting Lord.

GOETHE

154

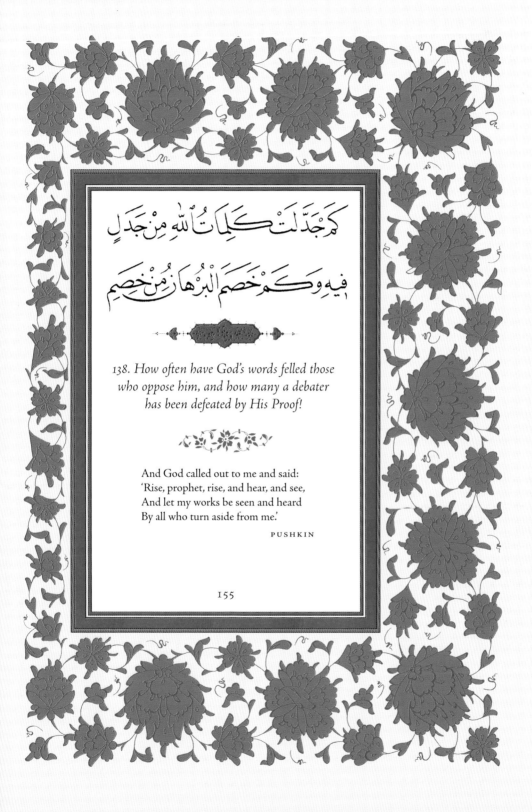

كَمْ جَدَّلَتْ كَلِمَاتُ اللهِ مِنْ جَدَلٍ

فِيهِ وَكَمْ خَصَمَ الْبُرْهَانُ مِنْ خَصِمٍ

138. How often have God's words felled those
who oppose him, and how many a debater
has been defeated by His Proof!

And God called out to me and said:
'Rise, prophet, rise, and hear, and see,
And let my works be seen and heard
By all who turn aside from me.'

PUSHKIN

155

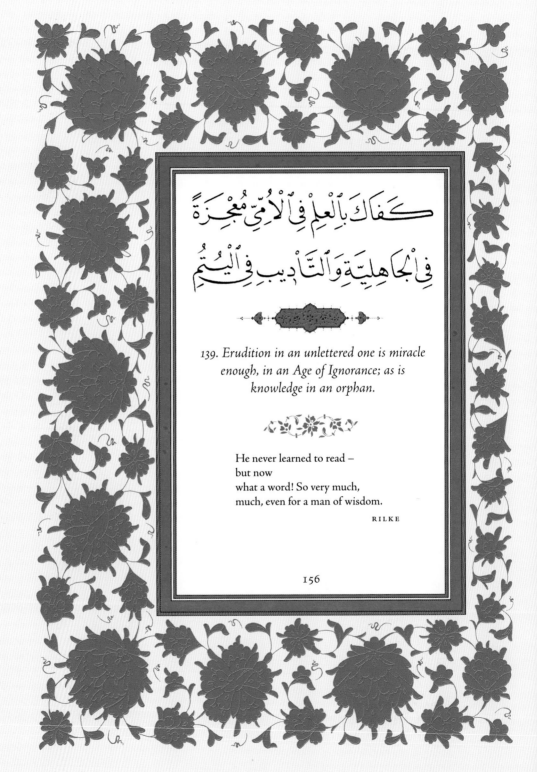

كَفَاكَ بِالْعِلْمِ فِى الْأُمِّىِّ مُعْجِزَةً
فِى الْجَاهِلِيَّةِ وَالتَّادِيبِ فِى الْيُتْمِ

139. *Erudition in an unlettered one is miracle*
enough, in an Age of Ignorance; as is
knowledge in an orphan.

He never learned to read –
but now
what a word! So very much,
much, even for a man of wisdom.

RILKE

156

خَدَمْتُهُ بِمَدِيحٍ اسْتَقِيلُ بِهِ
ذَنُوبَ عُمْرٍ مَضَى فِي الشِّعْرِ وَالْخَدَمِ

*140. By this eulogy have I served him,
hoping to be redeemed from the sins of a
life of odes and patronage.*

If the poet's reward
is the dust on your road,
he receives in each mote a new sun,
He has praised with his soul
the dust of your road,
Let him join it, magnanimous one!

ATTAR

157

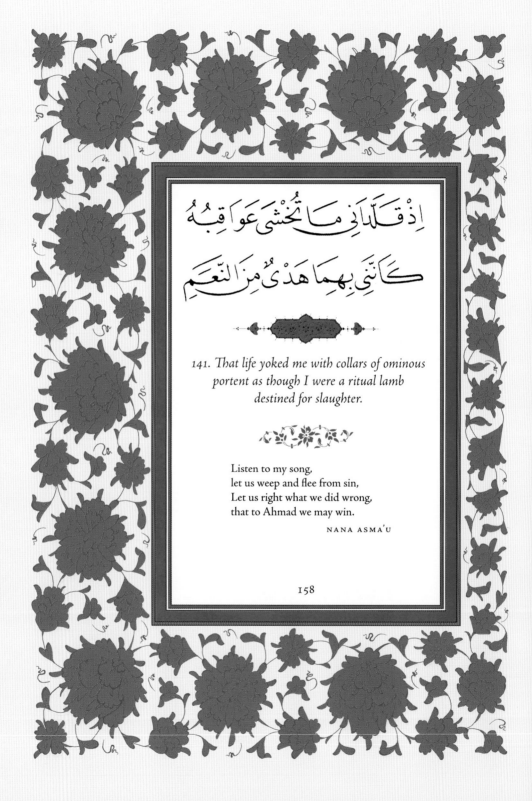

اِذْ قَلَّدَانِی مَا تُخْشَی عَوَاقِبُهُ

كَانَنِی بِهِمَا هَدْیُ مِنَ النَّعَمِ

141. *That life yoked me with collars of ominous*
portent as though I were a ritual lamb
destined for slaughter.

Listen to my song,
let us weep and flee from sin,
Let us right what we did wrong,
that to Ahmad we may win.

NANA ASMA'U

158

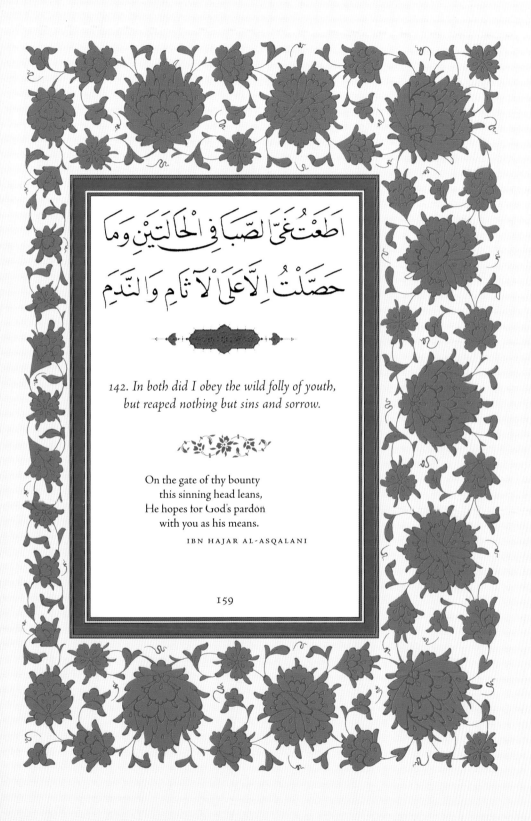

اَطَعْتُ غَيَّ الصَّبَا فِى الْحَالَتَيْنِ وَمَا
حَصَّلْتُ إِلَّا عَلَى لَا آثَامِ وَالنَّدَمِ

142. *In both did I obey the wild folly of youth,*
but reaped nothing but sins and sorrow.

On the gate of thy bounty
this sinning head leans,
He hopes for God's pardon
with you as his means.

IBN HAJAR AL-ASQALANI

159

فَيَا خَسَارَةَ نَفْسٍ فِي تِجَارَتِهَا

لَمْ تَشْتَرِ الدِّينَ بِالدُّنْيَا وَلَمْ تَسُمِ

143. *Such a loss to my soul was the deal that*
it struck! It didn't buy (or even seek to buy!)
the next world at this world's price.

While the best of creation you are,
the worst am I.
While master of both worlds you are,
the lowest am I.

MAWLANA MUHAMMAD NANOTVI

160

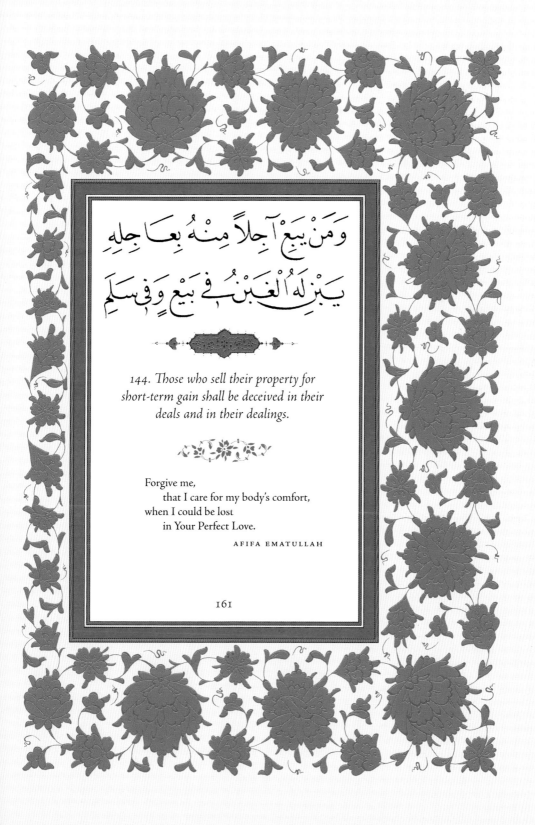

ومَنْ يَبِعْ آجِلاً مِنْهُ بِعَاجِلِهِ
يَبْزِلهُ الْغَبْنُ فِي بَيْعٍ وَفِي سَلَمٍ

144. *Those who sell their property for*
short-term gain shall be deceived in their
deals and in their dealings.

Forgive me,
    that I care for my body's comfort,
when I could be lost
    in Your Perfect Love.

AFIFA EMATULLAH

161

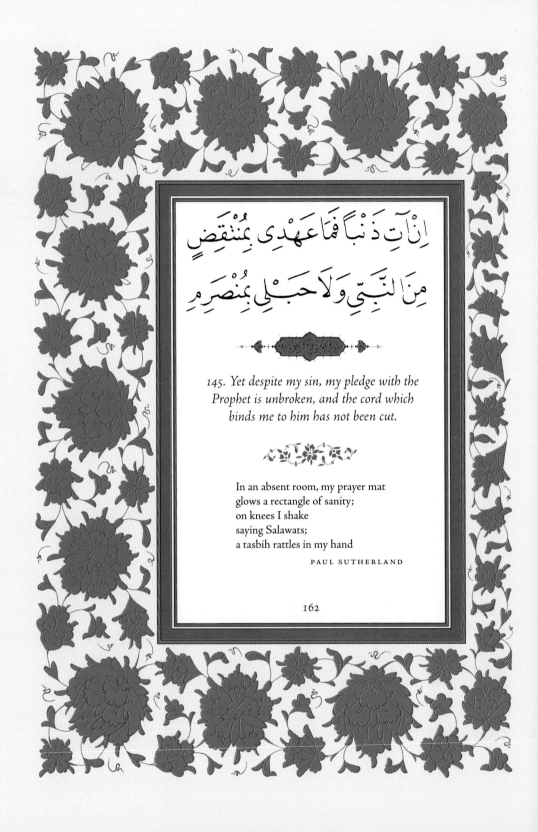

اِنْ آتِ ذَنْبًا فَمَا عَهْدِى بِمُنْتَقِضٍ

مِنَ النَّبِيِّ وَلَا حَبْلِى بِمُنْصَرِمِ

145. *Yet despite my sin, my pledge with the Prophet is unbroken, and the cord which binds me to him has not been cut.*

In an absent room, my prayer mat
glows a rectangle of sanity;
on knees I shake
saying Salawats;
a tasbih rattles in my hand

PAUL SUTHERLAND

162

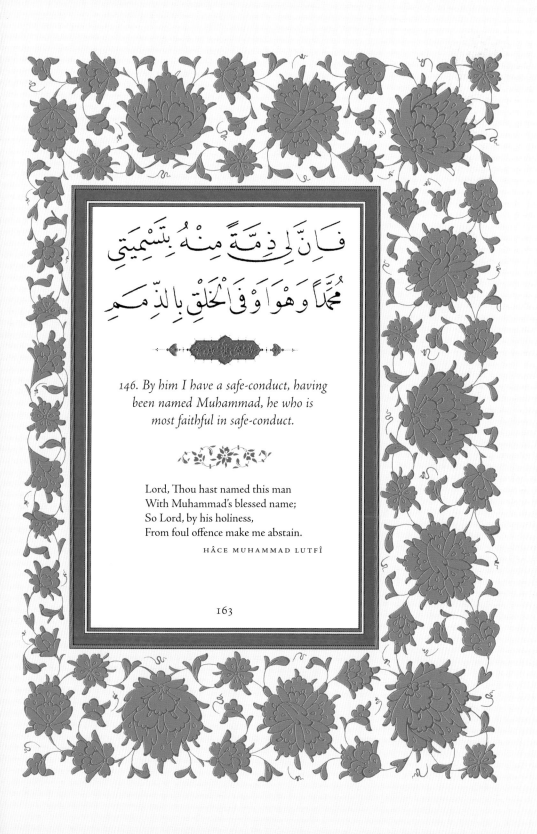

فَانَّ لِى ذِمَّةً مِنْهُ بِتَسْمِيَتِى

مُحَمَّدًا وَهُوَ أَوْفَى الْخَلْقِ بِالذِّمَمِ

146. *By him I have a safe-conduct, having*
been named Muhammad, he who is
most faithful in safe-conduct.

Lord, Thou hast named this man
With Muhammad's blessed name;
So Lord, by his holiness,
From foul offence make me abstain.

HÂCE MUHAMMAD LUTFÎ

163

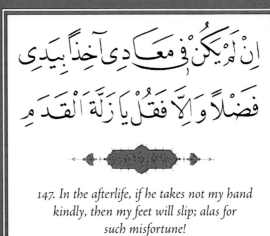

اِنْ لَمْ يَكُنْ فِى مَعَادِى آخِذاً بِيَدِى
فَضْلاً وَاِلاَّ فَقُلْ يَا زَلَّةَ الْقَدَمِ

147. In the afterlife, if he takes not my hand
kindly, then my feet will slip; alas for
such misfortune!

Though all things take their origin from There,
Do not resign yourself to Power's waves.
Of Ahmad's counsel let all men beware:
'Before the Master we must act as slaves!'

HAMZA FANSURI

164

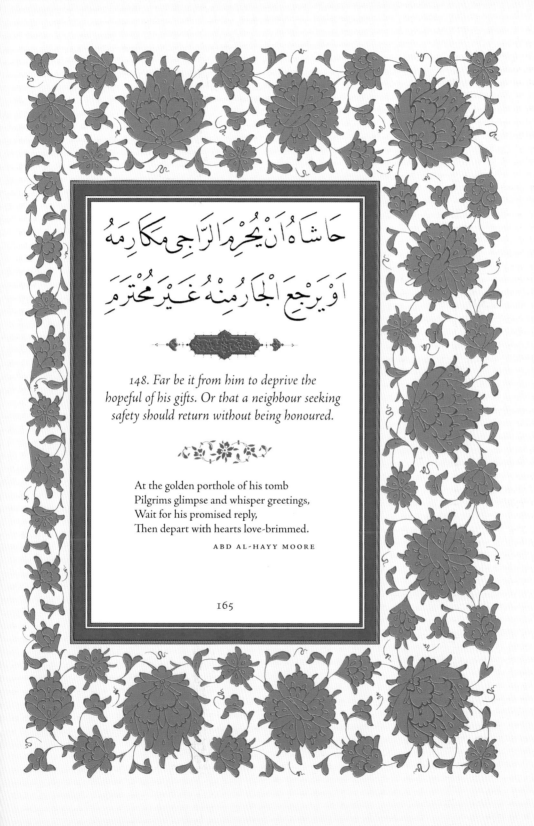

حَاشَاهُ اَنْ يُحْرِمَ الرَّاجِى مَكَارِمَهُ
اَوْ يَرْجِعَ الْجَارُ مِنْهُ غَيْرَ مُحْتَرَمِ

*148. Far be it from him to deprive the
hopeful of his gifts. Or that a neighbour seeking
safety should return without being honoured.*

At the golden porthole of his tomb
Pilgrims glimpse and whisper greetings,
Wait for his promised reply,
Then depart with hearts love-brimmed.

ABD AL-HAYY MOORE

165

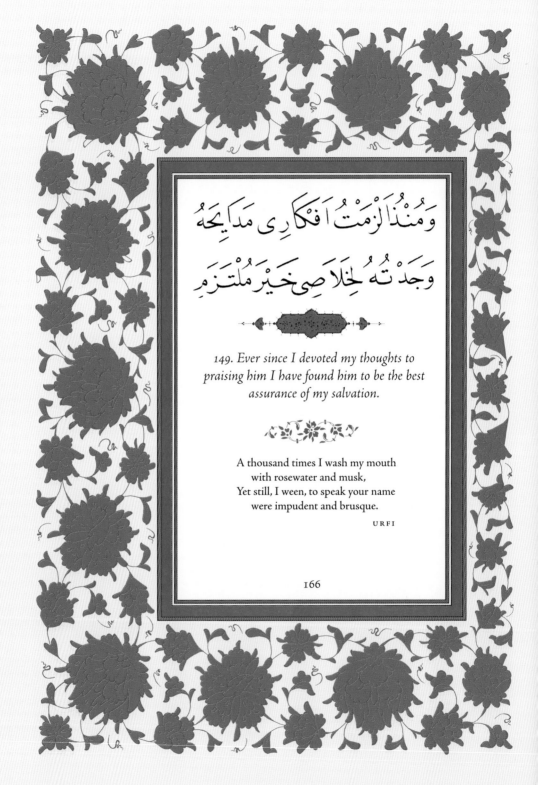

وَمُنْذُ اَلْزَمْتُ اَفْكَارِى مَدَايْحَهُ

وَجَدْتُهُ لِخَلَاصِى خَيْرَ مُلْتَزِمِ

149. *Ever since I devoted my thoughts to*
praising him I have found him to be the best
assurance of my salvation.

A thousand times I wash my mouth
with rosewater and musk,
Yet still, I ween, to speak your name
were impudent and brusque.

URFI

166

وَلَنْ يَفُوتَ مِنْهُ الْغِنَى يَدَا تَرِبَتْ

اِنَّا الْحَيَا تُنْبِتُ الْأَزْهَارَ فِى الْأَكَمِ

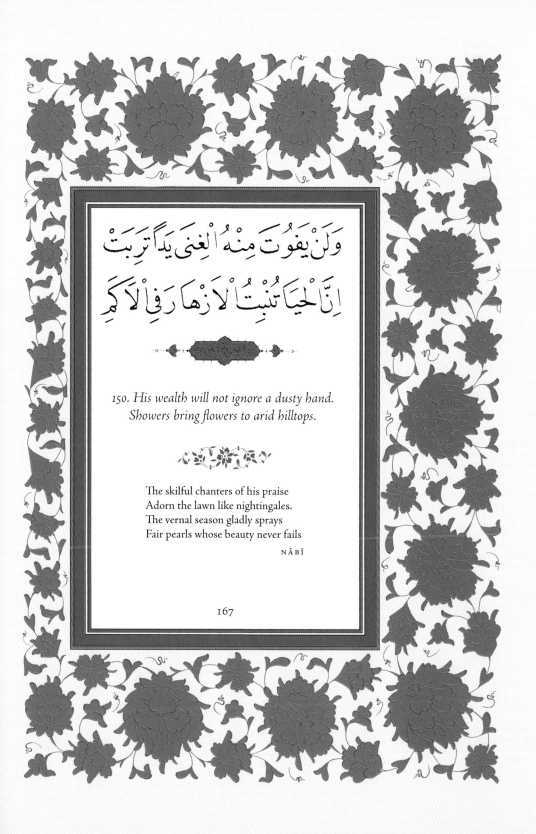

150. *His wealth will not ignore a dusty hand.*
Showers bring flowers to arid hilltops.

The skilful chanters of his praise
Adorn the lawn like nightingales.
The vernal season gladly sprays
Fair pearls whose beauty never fails

NÂBÎ

167

وَلَمْ أُرِدْ زَهْرَةَ الدُّنْيَا الَّتِي اقْتَطَفَتْ

يَدَا زُهَيْرٍ بِمَا أَثْنَى عَلَى هَرَمِ

151. *And yet I crave not the worldly flowers*
which the hand of Züheyr once picked by
praising Herem.*

The trusted of Prophets,
   the proof of the Way;
The king with no seal,
   no crown for his sway.

ATTAR

* Züheyr was a pre-Islamic poet; King Herem his patron.

يَا أَكْرَمَ الرُّسْلِ مَا لِي مَنْ أَلُوذُ بِهِ
سِوَاكَ عِنْدَ حُلُولِ الْحَادِثِ الْعَمِمْ

152. *Most noble of Messengers! To whom but
you shall I turn, when the General
Calamity befalls?*

By your standard may we pray,
when sky and earth are folded,
rivers and seas are voided,
mankind is resurrected,
on the latter day.

ANON.

169

وَلَنْ يَضِيقَ رَسُولَ اللهِ جَاهُكَ بِي
اِذَا الْكَرِيمُ تَجَلَّى بِاسْمِ الْمُنْتَقِمِ

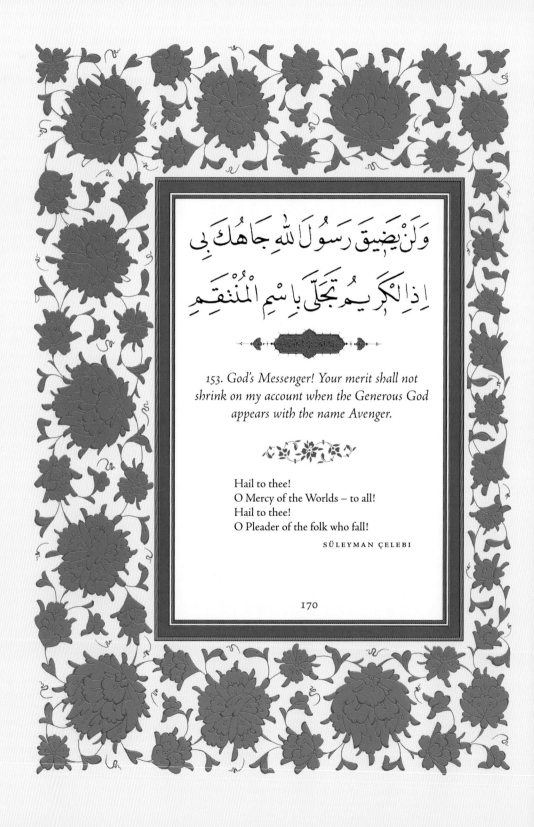

*153. God's Messenger! Your merit shall not
shrink on my account when the Generous God
appears with the name Avenger.*

Hail to thee!
O Mercy of the Worlds – to all!
Hail to thee!
O Pleader of the folk who fall!

SÜLEYMAN ÇELEBI

170

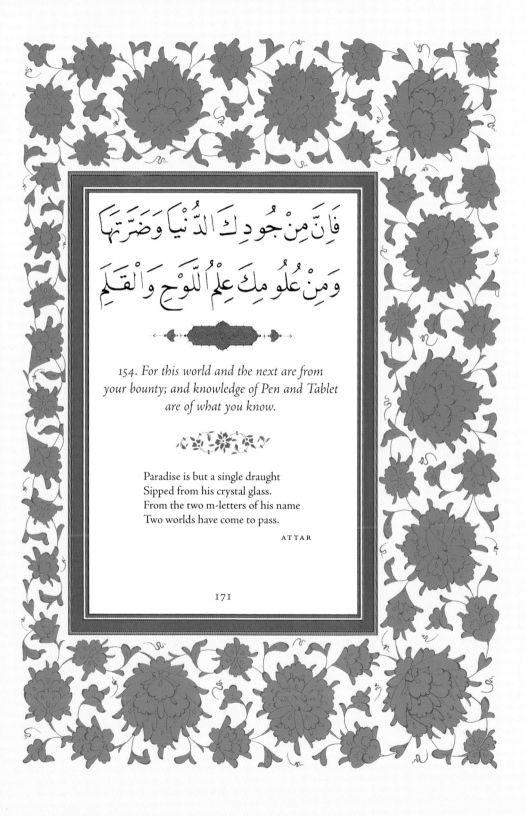

فَإِنَّ مِنْ جُودِكَ الدُّنْيَا وَضَرَّتِهَا

وَمِنْ عُلُومِكَ عِلْمُ اللَّوْحِ وَالْقَلَمِ

*154. For this world and the next are from
your bounty; and knowledge of Pen and Tablet
are of what you know.*

Paradise is but a single draught
Sipped from his crystal glass.
From the two m-letters of his name
Two worlds have come to pass.

ATTAR

171

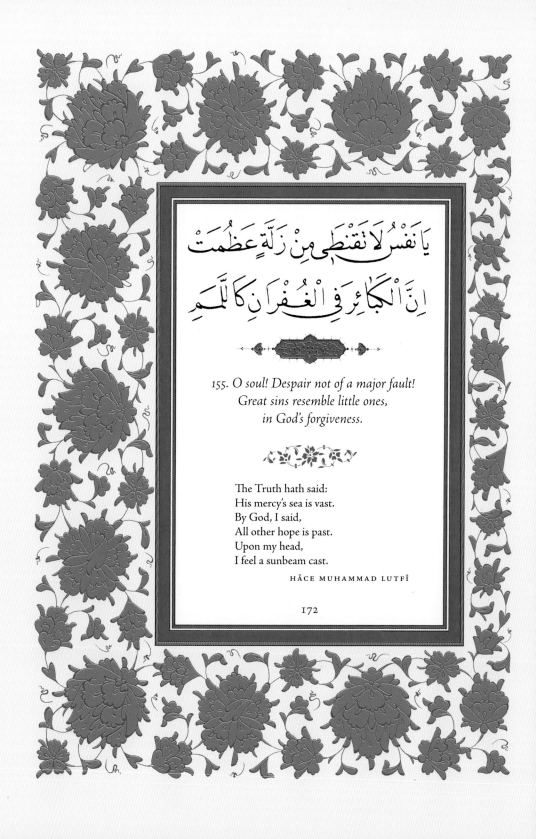

يَا نَفْسُ لَا تَقْنَطِى مِنْ زَلَّةٍ عَظُمَتْ

اِنَّ الْكَبَائِرَ فِى الْغُفْرَانِ كَاللَّمَمِ

155. *O soul! Despair not of a major fault!*
Great sins resemble little ones,
in God's forgiveness.

The Truth hath said:
His mercy's sea is vast.
By God, I said,
All other hope is past.
Upon my head,
I feel a sunbeam cast.

HÂCE MUHAMMAD LUTFÎ

172

لَعَلَّ رَحْمَةَ رَبِّي حِينَ يَقْسِمُهَا
تَأْتِي عَلَى حَسَبِ الْعِصْيَانِ فِي الْقَسْمِ

156. It may be, when my Lord distributes
His mercy, that it will come in proportion
equal to our sins.

Oh Allah, Ya Ra'uf
    only You can rescue me
from this habit of despair.
        Have pity, wash me from within.

AFIFA EMATULLAH

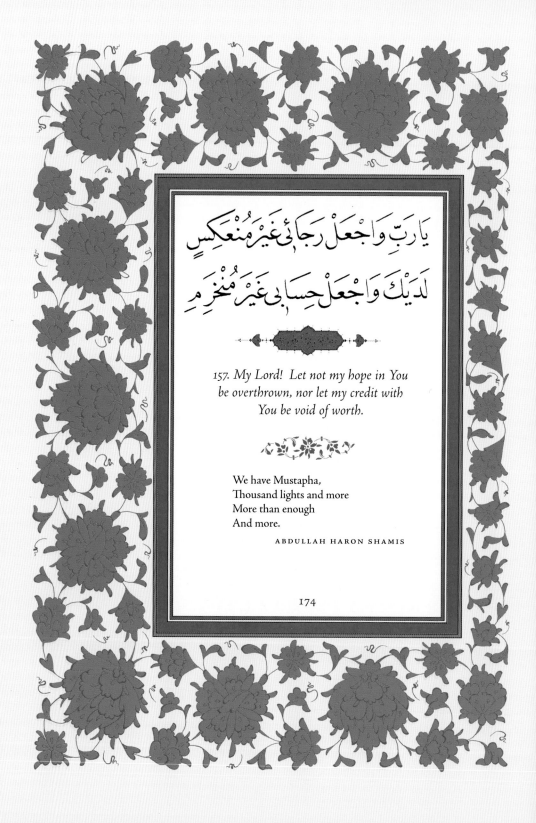

يَارَبِّ وَاجْعَلْ رجَائى غَيْرَ مُنْعَكِسٍ

لَدَيْكَ وَاجْعَلْ حِسَابى غَيْرَ مُنْخَرِمِ

*157. My Lord! Let not my hope in You
be overthrown, nor let my credit with
You be void of worth.*

We have Mustapha,
Thousand lights and more
More than enough
And more.

ABDULLAH HARON SHAMIS

174

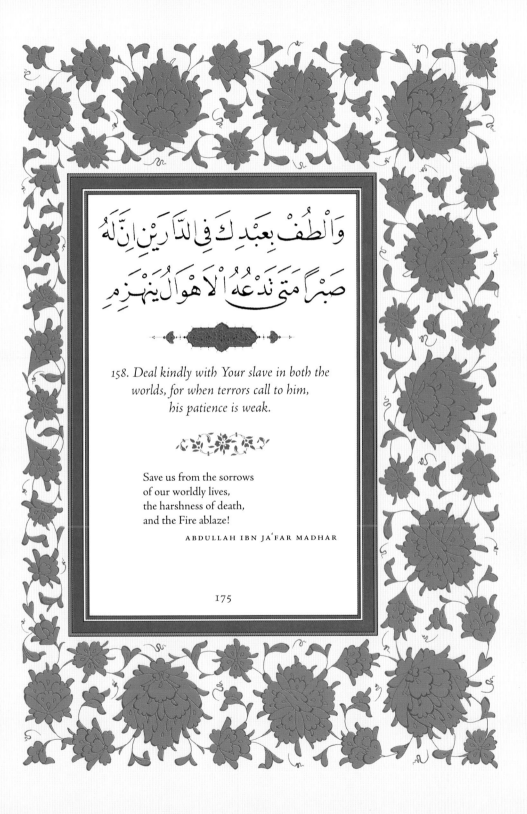

وَالْطُفْ بِعَبْدِكَ فِى الدَّارَيْنِ اِنَّ لَهُ

صَبْرًا مَتَى تَدْعُهُ الْأَهْوَالُ يَنْهَزِمِ

158. Deal kindly with Your slave in both the
worlds, for when terrors call to him,
his patience is weak.

Save us from the sorrows
of our worldly lives,
the harshness of death,
and the Fire ablaze!

ABDULLAH IBN JA'FAR MADHAR

175

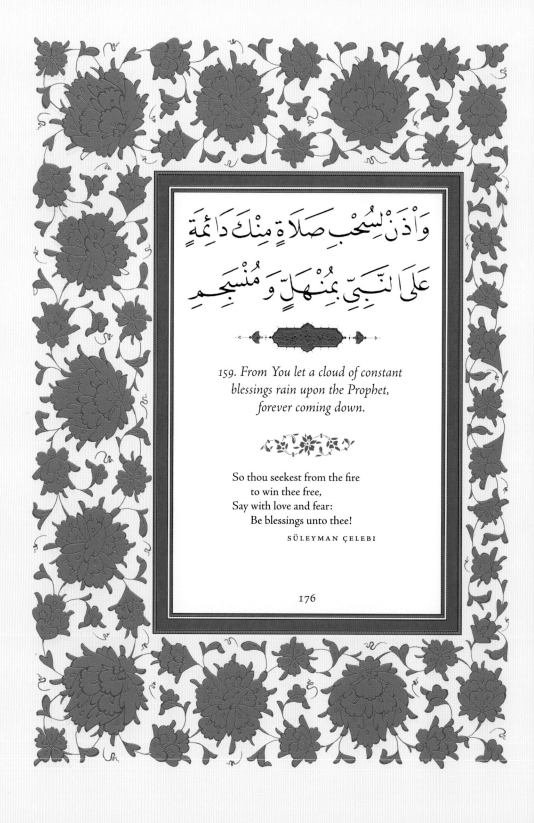

وَاْذَنْ لِسُحْبِ صَلَاةٍ مِنْكَ دَائِمَةٍ

عَلَى النَّبِيِّ بِمُنْهَلٍّ وَمُنْسَجِمِ

159. From You let a cloud of constant
blessings rain upon the Prophet,
forever coming down.

So thou seekest from the fire
to win thee free,
Say with love and fear:
Be blessings unto thee!

SÜLEYMAN ÇELEBI

176

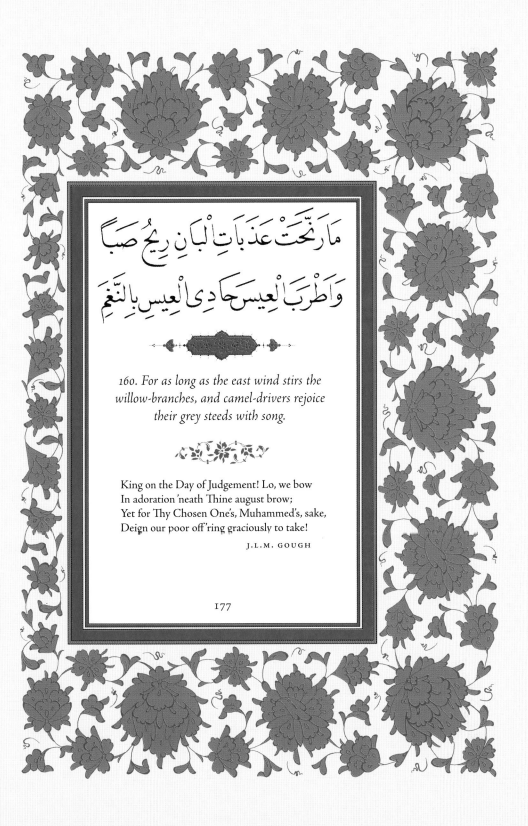

مَا رَنَّحَتْ عَذَبَاتِ الْبَانِ رِيحُ صَبَا

وَاَطْرَبَ الْعِيسَ حَادِى الْعِيسِ بِالنَّغَمِ

160. For as long as the east wind stirs the
willow-branches, and camel-drivers rejoice
their grey steeds with song.

King on the Day of Judgement! Lo, we bow
In adoration 'neath Thine august brow;
Yet for Thy Chosen One's, Muhammed's, sake,
Deign our poor off'ring graciously to take!

J.L.M. GOUGH

177

SOURCES

Translations are by the compiler unless otherwise stated.

Abdullah Haron Shamis (b.1974) Epsom. *English* 174
Abdullah ibn Ja'far Madhar (17th century) Hadramawt. *Arabic* 175
Abdullah Quilliam Bey (d.1932) Isle of Man. *English* 47, 80, 84, 114, 151
Abd al-Hayy Moore (b.1940) Philadelphia. *English* 55, 165
Afifa Ematullah (b.1952) Kingston. *English* 161, 173
Ahmed Shawqi (d.1932) Cairo. *Arabic* 78, 119
Ahmet Paşa (d.1497) Bursa. *Turkish* 121
A'isha al-Ba'uniyya (d.1516) Damascus. *Arabic* 59, 74, 86, 153
Ali ibn Abi Talib (d.661) Medina, Kufa. *Arabic* 42
Ameena Emily Lincoln (1899) Delhi. *English* 115
Amherst Tyssen (d.1930) London. *English* 51, 93, 95, 79, 138, 141, 146, 148
Attar (d.1220) Nishapur. *Farsi* 32, 46, 54, 60, 64, 123, 127, 132, 157, 168, 171
Aziz Mahmûd Hüdâyî (d.1628) Üsküdar. *Turkish* 91
Beatrice Mohamed (1913) London and Edirne. *English* 144
Emin Alzueta (b.1965) Motril. *Spanish* 89, 97, 120
Emperor Qiang-Long (d.1799) Beijing. *Chinese* tr. M. Broomhall 118
Faizi (d.1595) Delhi. *Farsi* 56
Firdawsi (d. *ca* 1026) Tus. *Farsi* tr. Arthur and Edmund Warner 61, 47, 66, 69
Fuzuli (d.1556) Baghdad. *Turkish* tr. Sofi Huri 20, 72, amended AHM 57, tr.
    AHM 81, 107
Ghalib (d.1869) Delhi. *Urdu* tr. Anon. 143
al-Ghazâli (d.1111) Tus and Baghdad. *Arabic* tr. A.J. Arberry 36, 39
Goethe (d.1832) Weimar. *German* tr. Maryam Williams 133, 154
Gough, J.L.M. (1897) Hamilton, Ohio. *English* 177
Hacı Bayram Velî (d.1429) Ankara. *Turkish* 49
Hâce Muhammed Lutfi (d.1956) Erzurum. *Turkish* 50, 163, 172
al-Haddad, Imam (d.1720) Tarim. *Arabic* 41, 63
Hamza Fansuri (d. *ca* 1600) Aceh. *Malay* tr. Selim May 104, 164
Hassân ibn Thâbit (d. *ca* 661) Medina. *Arabic* 58, 145, 147
Hibatullah Işân (d.1890) Kazan. *Tatar* 29
Hujvîrî (d.1072) Lahore. *Farsi* tr. Reynold Nicholson 38
Ibn 'Ata'illâh (d.1309) Alexandria. *Arabic* 34, 112
Ibn Daqîq al-'Id (d.1302) Yanbu' and Cairo. *Arabic* 17
Ibn Hajar al-'Asqalânî (d.1449) Cairo. *Arabic* 159
Ibn Hazm (d.1064). Cordoba. *Arabic* tr. A.J. Arberry, 117
Ibn Khaldûn (d.1406) Tunis etc. *Arabic* 53

Indrit Sinanaj (b.1980) Fier. *Albanian* tr. Rubin Hoxha 26
Iqbal (d.1938) Lahore. *Urdu* tr. Anon. 129
Izzet Mollâ (d.1829) Istanbul etc. *Turkish* tr. E.J.W. Gibb 24; tr. AHM 62, 94
Jamâli Kanboh (d.1536) Delhi. *Farsi* 128
Jâmî (d.1492) Herat. *Farsi* 65
Kadi Burhanettin (d.1398) Sivas. *Turkish* 22
Kaygusuz Abdal (d.1415) Elmalı and Cairo. *Turkish* 23
Kemâl Arûçi (d.1977) Skopje. *Turkish* 122
Khâqânî (d.1199) Tabriz. *Farsi* 102
Kozeta Boçi (b.1973) Berat. *Albanian* tr. Kozeta Boçi 21
al-Kumayt (d.743) Kufa. *Arabic* 31, 142
Leylâ Hanım (d.1848) Istanbul. *Turkish* 70
Lisân al-Dîn Ibn al-Khatîb (d.1374) Granada. *Arabic* 106
Mahmut Kaya (b.1945) Istanbul. *Turkish* 103
Mawlana Khâlid Baghdadi (d.1827) Süleimaniye – Baghdad. *Arabic* 40, 71
Mawlana Muhammmed Qâsim Nanotvi (d.1880) Deoband. *Urdu* tr. Anon.
   109, 160
Mesihi (d.1512) Prizren and Istanbul. *Turkish* tr. E.J.W. Gibb 149
Mir Ali Shir Qâniʻ (d.1788) Thatta. *Sindhi* tr. Anon. 96
Muhammad ibn al-Habib (d.1972) Meknes. *Arabic* 28
Muhammad Jamal al-Rifaʻi (b.1935) Jerusalem. *Arabic* 33, 43
Nâbî (d.1712) Urfa and Istanbul. *Turkish* 167
Nana Asmaʻu (d.1865) Sokoto. *Hausa* tr. Anon. 158
Nizami (d.1209) Ganjeh. *Farsi* 27, 73, 99, 105, 124, 135
Omar Fraser (b.1960) London. *English* 101
Paolo Urizzi (b.1951) Trieste. *Italian* 98, 100
Paul Sutherland (b.1947) Canada. *English* 45, 162
Pushkin (d.1837) Moscow. *Russian* tr. Babette Deutsch 155
Rilke (d.1926) Prague. *German* 110, 156
Riad Nourallah (1998) Beirut and London. *English* 92, 136, 139
Rumi (d.1273) Konya. *Farsi* 52, 76, 82, 113, 126
Rusmir Mahmutcehagić (b.1948) Sarajevo. *English* 131
Saʻdi (d. *ca* 1291) Shiraz. *Farsi* tr. A.J. Arberry 30, 44
Sanaʻi (d.1150) Ghazna. *Farsi* 68, 83
Süleyman Çelebi (d.1422), Bursa. *Turkish* tr. E.J.W. Gibb 75, 85, 88, 170, 176
Sünbülzâde Vehbi (d.1809) Istanbul. *Turkish* 77
Urfi (d.1592) Shiraz and Lahore. *Persian* 125, 166
Usman dan Fodio (d.1817) Sokoto. *Hausa* tr. Anon. 19, 90
Victor Hugo (d.1885) Paris. *French* tr. T. Viele 25
Wilfred Scawen Blunt (d.1922) Horsham. *English* 137, 152
Yahya Parkinson (d.1918) Kilwinning. *English* 18, 140, 150
Yûnus Emre (d.1320) Karaman (?). *Turkish* 108
Zâtî (d.1548) Istanbul. *Turkish* tr. E.J.W. Gibb 130

The Mosque and Tomb of Al-Busiri, Alexandria

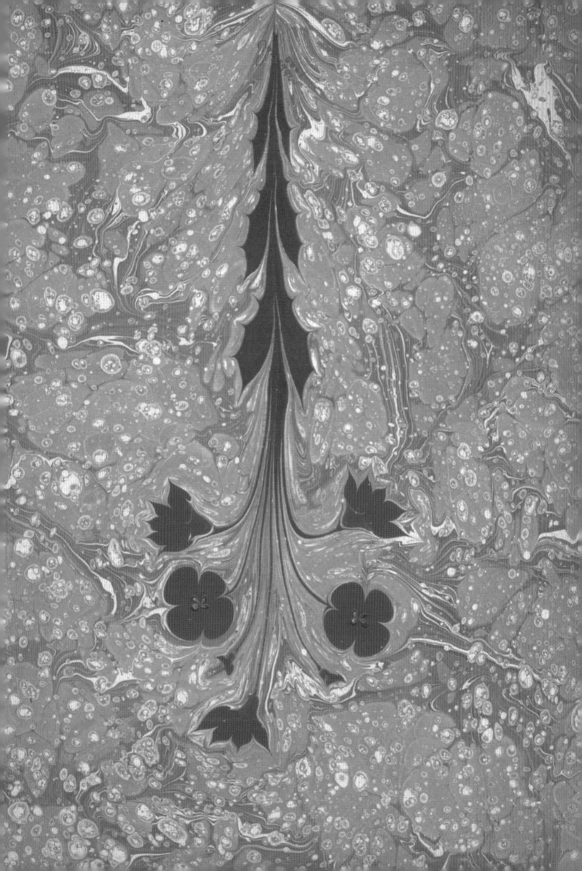